Praise for *The Financial Times Essential Guide to Developing a Business Strategy*

'I sincerely enjoyed reading this book. Vaughan Evans not only demystifies strategy, he provides a useful and enjoyable step-by-step guide to constructing effective business strategies. During my career I have witnessed and created hundreds of strategies, both good and bad. Applying these techniques will undoubtedly help produce more of the former than the latter.'

Jeff van der Eems, Chief Operating Officer, United Biscuits

'A wonderfully practical and highly readable guide to strategy development. Evans's Strategy Pyramid provides a simple but thorough framework, which he illustrates clearly through a step-by-step case study and many fascinating vignettes. Definitely worth working through.'

Marcus Alexander, Professor of Strategy and Entrepreneurship, London Business School

'The right strategy is key to business success, and yet most business leaders avoid thinking about or planning strategy. They fear that it needs the intellect of a nuclear physicist just to begin to design one. Vaughan Evans dispels this myth. He demonstrates clearly and concisely how anyone who is passionate about their business can develop a strategy that should serve them well.'

Guy Hands, Chairman and Chief Investment Officer, Terra Firma Capital Partners Ltd

'An excellent and very detailed handbook for anyone responsible for developing strategy'

Adrian Beecroft, Chairman, Dawn Capital and former Senior Managing Partner, Apax Partners

'This is the most succinct and most practical handbook on business strategy on the market. In just a couple of hundred well-written pages, it synthesizes the most important ideas in the field. What sets it apart – and brings it to life – is that every concept that is introduced is immediately illustrated in practice through the use of a real-life case study.'

Jules Goddard, Fellow, London Business School and author, with Professor Tony Eccles, of *Uncommon Sense, Common Nonsense: Why Some Organisations Consistently Outperform Others*

'If you are a small business or start up, this is an excellent guide to help you get your strategy right. Business strategy is all too often discussed in the context of big business. Vaughan Evans, on the other hand, makes it relevant to SMEs, demonstrating not only why but how to develop the right strategy to succeed.'

Anthony Karibian, CEO, bOnline Ltd. and serial entrepreneur

'A compelling insight into strategy development, one of the key success factors in every business'

Mike Garland, Partner and Head of Portfolio Group, Permira Advisers LLP

'A concise and highly practical guide to the fundamentals of strategic analysis and strategic planning.'

Robert M. Grant, ENI Professor of Strategic Management, Bocconi University, Milan, Visiting Fellow at Georgetown University, Washington, and author of *Contemporay Strategic Analysis*, now in its eighth edition

'This book will be a valuable addition to the armoury of the senior manager or advisor, offering a simple, concise and step-by-step guide to what is involved in setting an effective business strategy.'

Vince O'Brien, Director, Montagu Private Equity and former Chairman of the British Venture Capital Association

'Most big businesses and consulting groups have their own strategy development processes. Most, I am sure, are up to the task. But the beauty of this book is its simplicity. Evans believes that strategy should not be complex – otherwise how can one explain it, and its genesis, adequately to potential investors? Evans's Strategy Pyramid is a straight-forward, no nonsense approach to strategy development. Each stage is explained in a lucid and lively style and the reader is invited to follow an intriguing case study from start through to finish. It is a gem of a book.'

Christine Harvey, former Director of Business Analysis and Planning, GlaxoSmithKline R&D

'Vaughan Evans knows what investors need from a company. We look for long-term competitive advantage in markets where risk is manageable. In his previous book, *Key Strategy Tools,* he gave managers the full range of tools to choose from in building strategy. In this new book he sets out the most essential of those tools in the form of an uncomplicated DIY manual for the SME manager. It works perfectly.'

David Williamson, Managing Director, Nova Capital Management

'This is the perfect book for all company managers tasked with a requirement to develop and define the strategy for their business. Not only will they get clear guidance on how to go about it, but the resultant strategy will be one geared towards meeting the exacting demands of investors like ourselves. Invaluable.'

Bill Priestley, Managing Director, LGV Capital

'Vaughan Evans's recent *Financial Times Essential Guide to Writing a Business Plan* was invaluable in that he encouraged the planner to see the whole process through the eyes of the potential investor. He has used the same perspective in his new book on strategy development. Too often companies draw up their strategy on the hoof, with inadequate or inconsistent research and analysis. This book shows how to develop strategy with sufficient rigour to convince an external investor. And it does so simply, following an easily understandable process, the Strategy Pyramid. Every business, big or small, needs a strategy. Every entrepreneur or manager should follow this book.'

Stephen Lawrence, Chief Executive, Protocol Education Ltd and former Managing Director, Arthur D. Little

'This is the ideal companion to Evans's *The Financial Times Essential Guide to Writing a Business Plan*. A plan worthy of investment is only as sound as its underpinning strategy. This terrific little book shows the manager just what he or she needs to do to build that strategy. Where has this book been for the last fifty years?'

Jonathan Derry-Evans, Partner, Manfield Capital Partners

'A concise, precise and admirably practical guide for those starting or growing their own business and looking to apply sound logical principles to the task of strategic planning.'

Ben Johnson, Partner, Vitruvian Partners

'Vaughan Evans has earned a well deserved reputation for writing business books in straightforward everyday language, which are easy – and enjoyable – to read by busy managers. To borrow a phrase from his text, this book is not esoteric gobbledygook from an ivory tower in academia, but one based on the experience of a practitioner. It is from the same stable, and neatly complemented by, two of his earlier works – *Key Strategy Tools* and *The Financial Times Essential Guide to Writing a Business Plan*. In this latest book, Evans takes the reader through a series of logical steps to develop a strategy, with a central case study used as the "glue" throughout. To call the book a DIY manual may undervalue it, but it is that and more. It will be an enormous help to busy managers who are developing a business strategy for the first time, or trying to improve on previous attempts. This is another Evans book to be kept to hand on the desktop, not to be shelved!'

Grahame Hughes, Founding Director, Haven Power Ltd

'This is a great read. Vaughan Evans has written another compelling *Financial Times* guide. It is packed full of lively prose with highly practical tips and a great running case study. This should be a must-read for any entrepreneur or MD of a business of any size. I shall be using it in our own fund management business and shall invite all our investee companies to do the same.'

Peter Wright, Investment Director, Finance Wales

'This is a really good and practical guide – clear, insightful, straight-forward and practical. It is a must-have guide for anyone setting out to build or grow a business. If strategy can be likened to charting a wise and successful course though challenging waters, then Evans proves once again that he is a master mariner.'

James Courtenay, Global Head, Advisory and Infrastructure Finance, Standard Chartered Bank

'A straightforward and practical framework for developing your business strategy. Full of essential tips, tools and checklists, this book breaks down what can be a daunting task into a step-by-step guide that really works.'

Andrew Ferguson, Managing Director, UK Private Equity, Baird Capital

'This is a really practical guide to essential strategic positioning. The book complements superbly Evans's earlier *Key Strategy Tools* and provides managers with a clear and structured process in support of formulating, and owning, their appropriate organisational strategy, thereby building the confidence to execute it. I only wish this guidance had been written some 20 years ago, when launching

Eastern European enterprises into the world of strategic thinking and the competitive market economy.'

Gordon Gullan, Operations Director, Manet International Ltd

'Vaughan Evans is doing himself and his ilk out of the day job. With this easy-to-follow manual on how to develop a winning strategy, managers and investors won't need to engage pricey strategy consultants any more. Thanks!'

Ken Lawrence, Partner, Gresham Private Equity

'A seminal business strategy manual, as invaluable to the entrepreneur, manager or business advisor as to the student of strategic planning.'

James Pitt, Partner, Lexington Advisors UK Limited

'This is a highly practical, tool-based guide to developing and implementing strategy for any business. It is an enjoyable read, packed with colourful examples and case studies that bring the theory to life in a highly user-friendly manner.'

Paul Gough, Partner, STAR Capital Partners Ltd

'This is a very interesting and instructive book. I enjoyed the many examples of how to apply the various concepts outlined in the real world. Also, from the standpoint of an investor, if a management team of a potential investee company works with some of the frameworks outlined in this book, the business case presented is likely to be tighter and more credible, as it will be founded on a structured understanding of the market opportunity and the company's approach to it.'

Sotiris Lyritzis, private investor

'I have worked with many SMEs over the years for whom the importance of having a clear strategy was well understood but its construction a daunting and frustrating journey into unfamiliar territory. Vaughan Evans's clear, concise and accessible guide to the whats, whys and hows of strategy development will be a huge boon to such businesses. I highly recommend it to any entrepreneur or manager looking for a practical and experience-driven guide to help him or her through the process.'

Richard Kemp, Managing Partner, Sephton Capital

For execsy.com

The Financial Times Essential Guide to
Developing a Business Strategy

The Financial Times Essential Guide to
Developing a Business Strategy

How to use strategic planning to start up or grow your business

Vaughan Evans

PEARSON EDUCATION LIMITED
Edinburgh Gate
Harlow CM20 2JE
United Kingdom
Tel: +44 (0)1279 623623
Web: www.pearson.com/uk

First edition published 2013 (print and electronic)

© VEP (UK) Limited (print and electronic)

The right of Vaughan Evans to be identified as author of this work has been asserted by him in accordance with the Copyright, Designs and Patents Act 1988.

Pearson Education is not responsible for the content of third-party internet sites.

ISBN: 978-1-292-00261-3 (print)
 978-1-292-00281-1 (PDF)
 978-1-292-00280-4 (ePub)
 978-1-292-00586-7 (eText)

British Library Cataloguing-in-Publication Data
A catalogue record for the print edition is available from the British Library

Library of Congress Cataloging-in-Publication Data
Evans, Vaughan, 1951–
 The Financial times essential guide to developing a business strategy : how to use strategic planning or start up or grow your business / Vaughan Evans. -- 1st edition.
 pages cm
 Includes index.
 ISBN 978-1-292-00261-3 (pbk.)
 1. Strategic planning. 2. Business planning. I. Financial times (london, England) II. Title.
 HD30.28.E827 2013
 658.4'012--dc23
 2013031682

10 9 8 7 6 5 4 3 2 1
17 16 15 14 13

Cover image © Steve McAllister / Getty Images

Print edition typeset in 9pt Stone Serif by 3
Print edition printed and bound in Great Britain by Henry Ling Ltd, at the Dorset Press, Dorchester, Dorset

NOTE THAT ANY PAGE CROSS REFERENCES REFER TO THE PRINT EDITION

Contents

Acknowledgements

We are grateful to the following for permission to reproduce copyright material:

Figures 4.1 and 7.1 reprinted with the permission of The Free Press, a Division of Simon & Schuster, Inc., from *Competitive Strategy: Techniques for Analyzing Industries and Competitors* by Michael Porter. Copyright © 2004 by Michael Porter. All rights reserved; Figure 5.1 adapted from Ansoff, Igor H., 'Strategies for Diversification', *Harvard Business Review*, Sept-Oct 1957, courtesy of Harvard Business School Publishing; Figure 5.3 reprinted with permission of The Free Press, a Division of Simon & Schuster, Inc., from *Competitive Advantage* by Michael Porter. Copyright © 2004 by Michael Porter. All rights reserved; Figures 8.1 and 8.3 adapted from the BCG Portfolio Matrix from the Product Portfolio Matrix © 1970, The Boston Consulting Group.

All other figures are the author's own.

In some instances we have been unable to trace the owners of copyright material, and we would appreciate any information that would enable us to do so.

About the author

Vaughan Evans is an independent strategy consultant (**www. managingstrategicrisk.com**), specialising in strategy and business planning for corporate clients and strategic due diligence for private equity. His background is in micro-economics and corporate finance and this has helped shape his thinking that the key constituents to a backable business strategy are threefold: understanding the market context, honing a competitive edge and managing risk. These constituents form the backbone of this book, the main aim of which is to keep strategy simple for every manager and entrepreneur.

Vaughan worked for many years at international management and technology consultants Arthur D. Little and at investment bankers Bankers Trust Co. He is the author of a number of successful business books, including the highly acclaimed *Key Strategy Tools: The 80+ Tools for Every Manager to Build a Winning Strategy* (2012) and the best-selling *The Financial Times Essential Guide to Writing a Business Plan: How to Win Backing to Start Up or Grow Your Business* (2011).

An economics graduate from Cambridge University and an Alfred P. Sloan fellow with distinction of London Business School, Vaughan is a dynamic and inspirational speaker. One of his entertaining yet educational keynote speeches, *KISSTRATEGY,* is on keeping strategy simple, yet backable.

Introduction

> You have brains in your head. You have feet in your shoes. You can steer yourself in any direction you choose. You're on your own, and you know what you know. And you are the guy who'll decide where to go.
>
> *Dr Seuss*

In this section

- Why strategy?
- What is strategy?
- What is the output?
- What is the outcome?
- What is a strategic plan?
- What is strategic planning?
- The Strategy Pyramid
- Business vs corporate strategy

Why strategy?

As Dr Seuss says for the individual, so too for the company. You guys can steer your company in any direction you choose. You're on your own. You'll decide where to go, what strategy to pursue.

But what is it about the word 'strategy' that strikes awe into the souls of the manager or entrepreneur?

Does it conjure up daunting images of business school professors spouting smug, esoteric gobbledygook? Or of slick, suave, smooth-talking consultants doing their damnedest to give lawyers a good name?

It need not be like that. Strategy is for the manager. And for the entrepreneur. Strategy is for the ordinary person, the likes of you and me.

There should be no mystique over strategy. It is what you need to do to get your firm to the next level. That's all.

You are where you are. Strategy gets you to where you want to be.

You may be an entrepreneur, with an established firm or just starting out. Or you're the manager of a small or medium-sized company. Maybe you manage a division of a larger company.

Whichever, you need to know which direction your firm should head in. You need a strategy.

Without a strategy, you may still get to where you want to go. That's called luck.

With a strategy, you have a very much greater chance of getting there. That's sense.

But you may well need help. You don't need to go to business school or attend a business course at the local adult education college. Nor may you need an adviser. But you may need a guide.

There are thousands of documents, paper and electronic, to be found on business strategy – or on its many angles or models. They range from pamphlets to tomes.

But this is a book which does what it says on the cover. It is an *essential* guide to business strategy.

It tells you what you *need* to know to draw up a winning strategy for your firm. No more, no less. And it does so in a couple of hundred pages.

It makes no attempt to discuss all the various complex theories and models of strategy propounded by learned professors or business gurus. The tomes do that.

This book cuts to the chase. It sets out what works.

Strategy need not be complex. The process of building sustainable competitive advantage for the average firm, whether small, medium-sized or reasonably large, unlike admittedly for a global, multi-divisional, multi-country giant, can be straightforward – as long as you follow a proven, structured process.

This book gives you a simple framework, honed from years of experience, for drawing up a winning strategy for your firm. You won't need an adviser, a consultant, a mentor. Nor will you need a team of analysts.

All you need is this little book. And you.

Together we shall develop the strategy you need for your firm to succeed.

What is strategy?

Strategy is defined by the *Oxford English Dictionary* as 'a plan of action designed to achieve a long-term or overall aim'.

That says it all. You want to take your firm to the next level. You need a strategy to get there. You need a plan of action designed to achieve that aim of getting to the next level.

But there are more technical definitions, and many of them, ranging from the elaborate to the pithy – like General Sun Tzu's 'know your opponent' in the sixth century BC or Kenichi Ohmae's rather more recent 'in a word, competitive advantage' (that's actually two words, but who's counting?!).

And here is one from the undisputed strategy guru of the last four decades, Michael Porter: 'strategy is about ... choosing to be different'.

I am an economist by training, so I feel the need to bring the word 'resources' into the broader definition. Just as economics can be defined as the optimal allocation of a nation's scarce resources, so can a company's strategy be defined thus:

> *Strategy is how a company achieves its goals by allocating its scarce resources to gain a sustainable competitive advantage.*

Your strategy will set out how you plan to allocate your scarce resources to meet your goals. These resources are essentially your assets – your people, physical assets (for example, land, buildings, equipment and inventory) and cash (and borrowing capacity).

This book will guide you in how you should invest your firm's resources to optimal effect to gain a lasting competitive advantage – and thereby meet your goals.

What is the output?

So you develop a strategy for your business. What does it look like?

Is it a booklet? A document? A spreadsheet?

It can be any of these. But best is a short slide presentation. This format enables you to highlight conclusions in their starkest light.

The strategic conclusions may be preceded by 50+ slides of analysis, on demand, competition, the competitive gap and so forth (better, though, if all this detail is confined to an appendix), but when the conclusions arrive they will be emphatic, on just a slide or two. Do this, do that. They will be brief, bulleted and brutish – with no ifs and buts.

The output should be a clear road map on the direction the firm needs to travel over the next few years – succinct, punchy, memorable.

It is not an action plan. That is an altogether more detailed affair, with actions scheduled within a given timeframe – typically by the week, sometimes by the month, even by the day. An action plan may well form part of a strategic plan – see below.

A strategy is a planned *framework* for action. It is the background against which each task in an action plan should be judged. Each task must be consistent with the firm's strategy.

A strategy might conclude, for example, among other things, that the firm should expand the capacity of the manufacturing plant producing a major product line. That is one bullet in the strategy document. The resultant action plan, setting out how inventory needs to be built up and stored before part of the plant is cordoned off for construction work, how each phase of construction should proceed, and so forth, with each task given specific time delimitations, is a much more detailed affair.

A strategy must be a crystal clear route map, taken from a helicopter perspective.

What is the outcome?

The successful outcome of a strategy is the meeting of the firm's goals and objectives.

But developing a strategy is not like drawing up a business plan or project plan. The successful outcome of a business plan is often the agreement of the board or external financiers to authorise a round of funding. The successful outcome of a project plan is typically a go-ahead decision on the project.

A strategy does not have such a clear end-result, a go/no-go decision. It has a range of results, typically more difficult to pin down and often with mixed results.

A firm's objectives may include the raising of market share by 5% and of operating margin by 3%. If the strategy achieves a market share jump of 7% but a shrinking of operating margin by 1%, has it been successful? It is difficult to say – it could be deemed so if the share gain seems sustainable and the margin shrinkage temporary, but we would need more detail before we could conclude one way or the other.

The output of strategy is a route map to a destination. The successful outcome is getting there.

What is a strategic plan?

Strategy gives a helicopter view on direction. A strategic plan is a ground-level plan of attack. It represents the first step in strategy implementation.

It will include a high-level action plan – not a day-to-day or week-to-week plan, which is more the remit of strategy implementation and project planning, but at least an annual, perhaps a quarterly, summary of what is needed to translate strategy into action.

It gives greater detail on the deployment of resources. It sets out how cash and human resources will need to be allocated, where and when, to achieve the strategy. It includes a phased investment plan.

Chapter 10 delves more deeply into the composition of a strategic plan.

What is strategic planning?

Different people can mean different things by the term 'strategic planning' – not just business folk but business academics too. Terms like 'strategy development', 'strategy implementation', 'strategic planning' and 'business planning' are used loosely at times.

Chapter 11 looks at strategic planning in more detail, but for the purposes of this book I will define this and related terms as follows:

- Strategy – see the definition above on 'What is Strategy?'.
- Strategy development – the process under which a strategy is developed, one such being the 'Strategy Pyramid' in Part One of this book.
- Strategic plan – a plan setting out a firm's strategy as well as a high-level action plan on the deployment of resources.
- Strategic planning – the building of strategy development periodically into the firm's planning process (see Chapter 11).
- Strategy implementation – the drawing up of detailed action plans on putting the strategy into effect.

■ Business planning – the writing of outline plans on the allocation of resources and the financial implications of strategy, typically for transactional purposes, such as raising finance.

Systematised strategic planning, built into the planning and budgeting process, is more the preserve of larger companies. Strategic planning on a periodic basis (every three years, say) or on an *ad hoc* basis, when needed to raise finance or transfer ownership, is advisable for a business of any size – see Chapter 11.

The Strategy Pyramid

This essential guide introduces you to a straightforward, practical, proven strategy development process, termed the Strategy Pyramid.

It is made up of nine building blocks, ranging from Chapter 1, knowing your business, to Chapter 9, addressing risk and opportunity. It will be your guide in developing your firm's strategy, in allocating your firm's resources optimally to gain sustainable competitive advantage.

Let's consider how the pyramid is constructed. First you need to know your business. Where exactly do the sources of profit lie in the business? In other words, which are the product/market segments you serve and which make the greatest contribution towards operating profit? Business segmentation is the foundation for strategy analysis (see Figure 0.1).

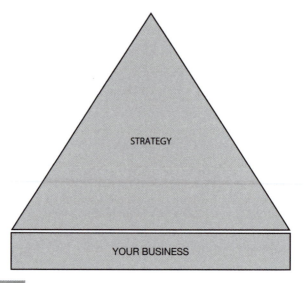

Figure 0.1   **Lay the foundation: know your business**

Once you've laid the foundation, the single most important factor in strategy development is to root it firmly within the context of the micro-economy in which your firm operates. Whatever key assumptions you make down the line on, for example, product development, pricing, service enhancement or cost reduction must reflect the reality of market demand and industry supply, today and tomorrow, in *your* micro-economy.

I have seen scores of strategies over the years built on inadequate research on the micro-economic environment. They are built on sand. Some succeeded, though they deserved not to. They succeeded through luck. Many faltered.

Micro-economic analysis must underpin the Strategy Pyramid (see Figure 0.2).

Figure 0.2 Set strategy on a micro-economic context ...

There are two distinct components of the micro-economy, market demand and industry supply, and they must be analysed separately. Failure to separate them can lead to muddled thinking. The tools used to analyse each component are entirely different. And both sets are equally important. Thus the micro-economy building block can be split in two (see Figure 0.3).

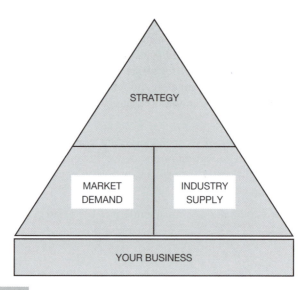

Figure 0.3   ... or a context of demand and supply

Within the context of the micro-economy, the crux of the strategy development process now rests on the analysis of your firm's competitiveness – how your firm measures against a whole range of factors critical to success. As many strategic insights will flow from this analysis of *internal* competitiveness as from the *external* micro-economic analysis (see Figure 0.4).

Figure 0.4   View strategy as the output of competitive analysis ...

Competitive analysis is best undertaken in two steps. The first is the current reality of how your firm stacks up to its peers in today's marketplace. And the second is how you envisage your firm rating against its competitors in the future – your target competitiveness. The competitive situation 'as is' and that 'to be' form two building blocks in the Strategy Pyramid (see Figure 0.5).

STRATEGY

COMPETITIVENESS:

CURRENT   TARGET

MARKET DEMAND   INDUSTRY SUPPLY

YOUR BUSINESS

Figure 0.5   ... both 'as is' and 'to be'

But there is something we have missed. How you see the future competitiveness of your firm depends partly, even largely, on what your aims for the firm are. What are your goals and objectives? To make a reasonable existence, to maximise profit growth, to keep your employees in their jobs, to satisfy a range of stakeholders? These overarching aims are fundamental to the strategy development process and belong to the foundation of the Strategy Pyramid (see Figure 0.6).

Figure 0.6   Target competitiveness also depends on your aims

Now is time to make an important distinction. There are two components to strategy: business and corporate. Business strategy is concerned with maximising the competitiveness of a single strategic business unit (see textbox or Chapter 6 for a full definition).

Figure 0.7   Strategy has two components: business and corporate

Corporate strategy is how you optimise your portfolio of businesses, whether through investment, acquisition or disposal, and how you add value to each through exploitation of your firm's overall resources and capabilities. The tools used for analysing business and corporate strategy are largely different, though there is overlap and some tools can be used for both. Unless yours is a single-business firm, you need to address both elements of strategy (see Figure 0.7).

We're almost there. Just one final building block is needed to complete the pyramid. The analyses of market demand, industry supply and your firm's competitiveness will encounter risk at every turn, likewise opportunity. Uncertainty is unavoidable and will be ever present. It must be addressed systematically in the strategy development process. It is core to success and should be wrapped around every part of the micro-economic and competitiveness analyses of the Strategy Pyramid (see Figure 0.8).

Figure 0.8   **Strategy development is wrapped in uncertainty**

The building blocks of the Strategy Pyramid now emerge, numbered 1 to 9 (see Figure 0.9).

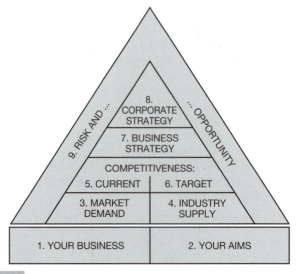

Figure 0.9   The nine building blocks of the strategy pyramid

All that remains is to convert the building block headings into task-oriented clauses and we have the first nine chapter headings for this book:

1. Knowing your business
2. Setting goals and objectives
3. Forecasting market demand
4. Gauging industry competition
5. Tracking competitive advantage
6. Targeting the strategic gap
7. Bridging the gap: business strategy
8. Bridging the gap: corporate strategy
9. Addressing risk and opportunity

Each chapter will set out the essential tools and techniques you need to build the block.

Finally, may I welcome you to the strategy development process. I hope you find the Strategy Pyramid both useful and stimulating. My purpose is to write a practical but lively guide to help you build the strategy you need for your firm to succeed.

Business vs corporate strategy

One thing we need to address upfront is how this book approaches the two distinct but related fields of strategy, business strategy and corporate strategy. A business, or, more technically, a strategic business unit ('SBU'), is defined as an entity with a closely interrelated product (or service) offering and a cost structure largely independent of other business units. Thus, in a large corporation, an SBU may well have not only its own CEO, CFO, COO, CSMO and CIO, but its own CTO, head of all R&D in that SBU.

An SBU is a substantive enough entity to warrant drawing up its own strategy, independent of strategies its fellow SBUs may be drawing up.

SBU strategy is known more simply as business strategy.

Corporate strategy is in the first instance how you allocate resources between your SBUs. Which will you invest in, which will you hold for cash generation, which will you sell, which may you be forced to close down? This is corporate strategy as portfolio planning.

But corporate strategy is more than that. It is about how you strive to attain synergies between your SBUs, how you create value in the centre, how you initiate a winning culture or capability that permeates the entire organisation. This is the resource-based theory of corporate strategy.

Most of this book is about business strategy. The Strategy Pyramid is essentially a business strategy tool, right up to Chapter 7 and including Chapter 9. Each step of the process can be followed by a single SBU.

Corporate strategy is addressed in Chapter 8.

The differentiation between corporate and business strategy can be temporary. Large corporations often spin off an SBU, whether through IPO, MBO or trade sale. That SBU becomes its own entity, NewCo, and may decide to set up its own SBUs, based on the key product/market segments formerly analysed in its business strategy. What used to be NewCo's business strategy is now corporate strategy. Furthermore, NewCo may in time decide to hive off one of its newly created SBUs, which then becomes its own entity, and so on.

Some of the more important strategy tools can be used for both business and corporate strategy, for example the Attractiveness/ Advantage matrix. For business strategy, the matrix can be used to assess a business's portfolio of product/market segments (see Chapter 6), while for corporate strategy, the same matrix can again be used to assess the overall firm's portfolio of businesses (Chapter 8).

Essential case study

Extramural Ltd Strategic Review, 2013

Extramural Ltd is a fictional case study used throughout this book. It is drawn from an industry I dipped in and out of a few times in the early 2000s and found fascinating. There can be few other industries which give so much joy so regularly to so many, where the end-customer is almost guaranteed to leave not just having learnt something useful, whether in education or a life skill, but with the broadest grin spread across his or her joyful young face.

It is the market for school activity and educational tours. Extramural Ltd is not modelled on any one player currently or formerly operating in this industry, but there will inevitably be aspects of Extramural which will strike a chord with certain players. It is a composite enterprise, created to reflect the industry as a whole and to highlight some of the more illuminating strategic challenges faced by many of its players.

This Extramural Ltd was started in 1992 by a young couple, Richard and Jane Davies, both of whom had over 10 years' prior experience of working in the package tour business – Richard in ski tours and Jane in the young adult market. Operating initially from just the one, small leased site near Totnes in Devon, Extramural has grown steadily to become one of the major players in the school activity tour business, operating out of 10 large, regionally spread sites, two of which are on the Continent. It has also become a significant player in educational tours and dipped its toes into the day camp business.

The Davieses have recently reached their 'Big Five-O' and have been pondering their future. They still own a majority shareholding in the company, but spy no interest among their two children to take it on – with one favouring medicine and the other treading the boards. They have received approaches from a number of parties representing competitors, both UK and foreign, and are frequently fêted by private equity houses.

They know full well that their shareholding is worth a lot of money, but they suspect it could be worth quite a bit more. They feel they owe it both to themselves and to their children to maximise shareholder value prior to exit in three to five years' time.

Extramural, now based in Exeter, Devon's charming capital city, turns over £20.5 million and enjoys an operating margin of 17.5%, yet the Davieses feel that the business exhibits notable elements of under-performance:

- Sales in the main business of school activity tours have been flat in recent years and margins, while healthy, are below those of the market leader.

- Margins in educational tours are lower, well below those of the market leaders, and the Davieses wonder whether this business may be stuck in the middle of the road, vulnerable to being run over.

- The new day camp business seems promising, but Extramural is as yet a small, me-too player.

They resolve to undertake a strategic review of their company. They contemplate engaging the services of an outside consultant, but they are only too aware of the unflattering definition of the latter: someone who borrows your watch to tell you the time.

There is no rush. The company is in no trouble. They decide to read their own watches and take on the strategic review themselves, assisted only by Sasha, their short-term intern, a bright, vivacious, enthusiastic young graduate in geography from Durham University, and, invaluably, by a recently acquired DIY guide to business strategy from the FT Essential Guide series ...

Strategy development

1

Knowing your business

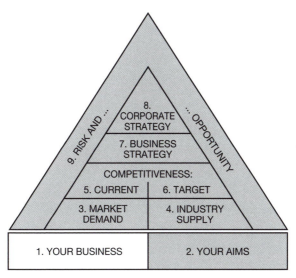

8. CORPORATE STRATEGY

9. RISK AND ...   **... OPPORTUNITY**

7. BUSINESS STRATEGY

COMPETITIVENESS:

| 5. CURRENT | 6. TARGET |

| 3. MARKET DEMAND | 4. INDUSTRY SUPPLY |

| 1. YOUR BUSINESS | 2. YOUR AIMS |

❝❝ Real knowledge is to know the extent of one's ignorance.

Confucius

In this chapter

- ▥ Identifying key segments
- ▥ Segmentation in a start-up

How well do you know your business? In which cupboards do the profits reside?

This is the essential starting point in strategy formulation. You need to know your business. You need to clarify the major business segments you compete in and which contribute most to the bottom line. Only when you have a clear perspective on which business segments are material to your firm's strategy should you proceed.

If your business is a start-up, the same applies. But we'll start with identifying key segments in an established business.

Identifying key segments

Does your firm serve some segments where you generate good sales but frustratingly little profit? And what of those merrier segments where sales are modest but margins meaty?

Step 1 in building block 1 of the Strategy Pyramid is to know your business, where the profit resides.

There are two components to this:

- Which business segments does your firm compete in – which products (or services, referred to in this chapter as just 'products') do you sell to which sets of customers?
- Which of these segments delivers the most profit?

Only once this segmentation process is complete should you embark on developing your strategy. There is no point in devoting hours of research, whether in analysing competitor data or gathering customer feedback, in a segment which contributes to just 1% of your operating profit – and which offers little prospect of growing that contribution over the next five years.

How you could strengthen your capabilities in that segment may be fascinating, but is not material to your business strategy and is of little interest to your board or backer.

You need to devote your time and effort to strengthening your firm's presence in those segments that contribute, or will contribute, to 80% or more of your business.

First, then, what is your business mix? What products or services does your business offer and to which customer groups? Which count for most in your business?

Businesses seldom offer just the one product to one customer group. Most businesses offer a number of distinct products to a number of distinct customer groups.

A product tends to be distinctive if the competition differs from one product to another. Some competitors may offer all your services; others may specialise in one or two of them. Others still may offer just the one as a spin-off to a largely unrelated business.

A customer group is distinctive if the customers have distinct characteristics and are typically reachable through distinct marketing routes.

Thus a customer group can be defined by who they are (e.g. leisure or business visitor, young or old, well or less educated), what sector they are in (especially for business-to-business ventures), where they are located (e.g. town or suburbs, region, country) or in other ways where different marketing approaches will be needed to reach them.

Each distinct product offered to a distinct customer group is a segment termed, in rather ungainly business-speak, a 'product/market segment' or, more simply, a 'business segment'.

If your business offers two products to one customer group, you have two business segments. If you stick with the same two products but develop a new customer group, you'll have four segments. Introduce a third product and sell it to both customer groups and you have six segments.

How many products does your business offer? To how many customer groups? Multiply the two numbers together and that's how many business segments you serve.

Now, which two, three or four segments are the most important? Which contribute most to sales? (Let's assume to start with that each segment has a similar cost profile, so the proportionate contribution to operating profit is the same as for sales.)

And will these same segments be the main contributors to sales over the next few years?

Set this out precisely and succinctly here. In too many strategic plans this basic information is absent. Often one sees a pie chart or two of sales by main product line, or sales by region or country, but what is left out is:

■ Sales by product/market segment – that is, sales of a specific product line *to a specific customer group*

■ That same information over time, say over the last three years.

Let's take a simple example. Your company makes widgets, small, medium and large, which you sell to three sectors, manufacturing, engineering and construction, in each of two countries, the UK and France. You operate in 3 × 3 × 2 = 18 product/market segments.

By far your biggest segment is large widgets to UK engineering, which account for 40% of sales. This is followed by medium widgets to UK engineering at 25% of sales and large widgets to French manufacturing at 15% of sales. Together these three segments account for 80% of sales. The remaining 15 segments account for just 20% of sales – see Figure 1.1.

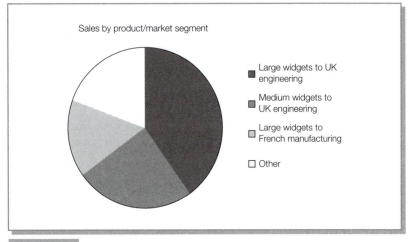

Figure 1.1 Key segmentation: an example

Very often, what would be set out here would be a pie chart showing a breakdown of sales by widget size – large, medium and small. Alongside might lie another pie chart showing sales by country, namely the UK and France. Better, it might combine both country and end-user data, breaking down sales into four customer groups: UK engineering, UK manufacturing, French engineering and French manufacturing.

This is useful information, but what would be even more useful would be a pie chart showing the real product/market segmentation as set out above. It would show one segment alone – large widgets to UK engineering – accounting for 40% of sales and another for 25%.

That would show that the key issues impacting on your firm's strategy development, whether relating to market demand, competition or your firm's competitiveness, are those pertaining to *one* particular segment – large widgets to UK engineering. Not large widgets in general, not small widgets, not the UK as a whole, not all of France, not French engineering, not UK construction, but specifically one product/market segment – large widgets to UK engineering.

Engineering customers will have different demand influences from those in construction. The UK may be at a different stage in the economic cycle to France. French engineering companies may have different solutions favouring medium over large widgets. Small widget producers may be more numerous and have more flexible, short-run production facilities than those making large widgets.

For any or all of these reasons, you need to know that one product/ market segment, large widgets to UK engineering, matters most in your business. And what matters next is the segment of medium widgets to UK engineering, followed by large widgets to French manufacturing.

And what of the future? Perhaps you are set to launch an extra-large widget tailored to the UK aerospace sector, which, if all goes to plan, could account for 20% of sales in three years' time.

So let's have a second pie chart alongside the first, showing forecast sales by main product/market segment in three years' time.

That, then, is the first step in the segmentation process – breaking up your business into the most useful product/market segmentation. The second step is to determine the profitability of each. In which segments do profits reside? Which contribute most to your firm's overall profit?

We need to repeat the exercise examining each segment's contribution not to sales, but to operating profit. That data may not exist. You surely have sales by product/market segment and probably gross profit too.

But it is operating profit or at least contribution to fixed overheads that we need. Some segments will be heavier consumers of the marketing budget or travel expenses than others.

The data that emerges from your management information system probably won't give this level of detail. In that case you should make estimates. Reasoned estimates are far better than no data. After all, you will soon be making reasoned judgement on a whole range of external factors, like market demand and industry competition, in drawing up your strategy.

The contribution of key segments to operating profit will differ from that for sales. Some segments will be more profitable than others. More profitable segments will have a higher share of operating profit than sales.

But that doesn't mean that the breakdown by operating profit is necessarily more useful than that by sales. The latter can be useful in highlighting where profitability in certain segments is lagging behind others and potentially how that gap can be narrowed.

Essential tip

Be careful of paralysis through analysis. Don't end up with dozens of segments. Concentrate on the half-dozen or so product/market segments that truly drive your firm's profit.

Let's go back to the example of the engineering company, where the segment of large widgets to UK engineering contributes to 40% of sales. Suppose the contribution to operating profit was only 30%, the same as that of the second-largest segment (in terms of sales), medium widgets to UK engineering – despite the latter contributing to only 25% of sales.

Both sets of data are important. There may be structural factors influencing the disparity in profitability – the large widget business may face competition from Far Eastern imports, unlike with medium widgets. This will limit the firm's choice of strategic options.

But it may be that the firm's manufacturing efficiency has fallen behind that of its domestic competitors, which have invested in capital equipment ideally suited for the larger widgets. This will lie within the firm's scope for action.

In summary, break down your business into the most important product/market segments and set out the contribution of each segment to both sales and operating profit. Do this for the business as it is today, consider how it has changed from three years ago, and project how it seems likely to change over the next three years.

Now you'll have the base knowledge of your business upon which to develop a strategy.

Essential tip

Now you have figured out which product/market segments matter most for your business, try brainstorming on what issues matter most in each of the main segments.

What is the key question you are trying to answer in your strategy development process? To answer that, what other questions need answering, especially those relating to certain rather worrying risks or exciting opportunities?

And to answer them, what more questions need answering?

Do this issue analysis right at the start of the strategy development process. Then proceed with the research and analysis needed to answer the key questions.

Essential example

Apple's saviour segments

What will be the next Apple blockbuster product? Will there be one?

In the 1990s Apple was a manufacturer of personal computers, one with a devoted following, but not large enough to prevent it from struggling financially. Sales started to decline in 1995 and were not to reach those levels again until 2005, during which time it recorded either low or negative profitability.

Yet by August 2012 Apple had become the most valuable company in history, reaching a stupefying market capitalisation of $619 billion, topping the record held by former rival Microsoft of $616 billion in December 1999.

A segmentation of Apple's business in the late 1990s would have shown a broad range of Macintosh personal computers, categorised perhaps by product, user type and region. The Macintosh was facing tougher competition from IBM and its many clones, now with an improved graphical user interface and running a superior operating system, Microsoft. Market share was eroding.

One new segment showed promise – a personal digital assistant, the Newton. Another was even more embryonic – a portable digital audio player, to be called the iPod, to link it to the promising flashy redesign of the Macintosh, the iMac.

The iPod turned the tide and led to iTunes, a revolution in music industry online distribution which has experienced exponential growth ever since. Apple recorded its 25 billionth track download in February 2012 – and some observers expect the 50 billionth to be registered before the end of 2013!

Then came the iPhone, a device which blended stylistically the capabilities of mobile phone, digital audio/video player and digital camera. More recently Apple launched the iPad, a tablet computer which seemed destined to cannibalise other lines but succeeded in creating its own category.

Personal computers now comprise just 15% of Apple's sales (year ended 29 September 2012), of which the 1990s stalwart of Macintosh desktops is a mere 4%. Over half of sales come from iPhone and related products and services, which have largely cannibalised the iPod (down to 4%). The new iPad category, just 8% in 2010, has leapt to 21%.

Apple grew net sales in 2010–12 from $65 billion to $157 billion – an average of 55% per year, which is the sort of growth rate more usually found at a start-up technology company. That a large global corporation can grow at such a rate is phenomenal and unprecedented.

But Apple missed its sales forecasts of iPhone units during Christmas 2012. Its share price tumbled.

Drawing up Apple's strategy for the next few years will not be easy. How to withstand competition from Samsung and others in the smartphone market will be tough enough, but what about the next big thing? Apple's strategists will need to take extra care with segmentation. Which product will be the next iPod, iPhone or iPad? That a smart television is in the pipeline, perhaps the iTV, is no secret, but can it be sufficiently differentiated in an already crowded market? What about an iWatch? How should Apple allocate resources accordingly? An iPhantastic challenge.

Segmentation in a start-up

If you are planning a business start-up, you may still need to segment. If you are to launch just the one product (or service) to one group of customers, fine, you won't need to segment any further. But are you sure you'll only have one product? One customer group?

Try categorising your products. And your customers. Is further segmentation meaningful? If so, use it. If not, don't waste time just for the sake of seeming serious. Stick to the one product for the one customer group, i.e. one business segment.

But there is one big difference. No matter how you segment, no matter how many customer groups you identify, they are all, at present, gleams in the eye.

You have no customers. Yet.

Your product must be couched in terms of its benefits to the customer. That is the business proposition. Not the way in which your product can do this, do that, at this price. But in the way in which your product or service can *benefit* the target customer.

Who is the target customer? In which way will he or she benefit from your offering?

And that is just in the one segment. Are there others?

Segmentation may lie at the very heart of your business proposition. It may have been in the very act of segmentation that you unearthed a niche where only your offering can yield the customer benefit. And you have since tailored your offering to address this very niche, this customer benefit.

For further stimulating thoughts on this, see the section on 'Will the fish bite?' in John Mullins' indispensable guide to business start-ups, *The New Business Road Test: What Entrepreneurs and Executives Should Do Before Writing a Business Plan.*

Here is a slightly different way of looking at it. Does your offering address some 'unmet need' in the marketplace? Does it fill a gap in a target customer's needs? This is one of the secrets to a new venture's success highlighted by William Bridges in his book, *Creating You & Co.* He suggests that an 'unmet need' could be uncovered by spotting signs such as a missing piece in a pattern, an unrecognised opportunity, an underused resource, a signal event, an unacknowledged change, a supposedly impossible situation, a non-existent but needed service, a new or emerging problem, a bottleneck, an interface, or other similar signs.

However you define the customer benefit, whether in terms of unmet needs or in a way more meaningful to your offering, you need to undertake some basic research to dig up whatever evidence you can glean of likely customer benefit.

An understanding of the differing elements of customer benefit will help you clarify segmentation in your start-up.

Essential case study

Extramural Ltd Strategic Review, 2013

Chapter 1: The business

Richard and Jane Davies start their strategic review on page one: segmentation. That's easy, they think. Extramural is evidently a firm in three distinctive segments – school activity tours, educational tours and day camps.

But hang on, says Jane. Are these segments or businesses? And does it matter?

They turn to the definition of a business, or a 'strategic business unit' (see the introduction to this book). This is an entity with a closely interrelated product offering and a cost structure largely independent of other businesses – it could viably have its own CEO and its own strategy.

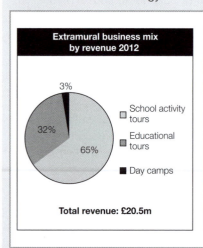
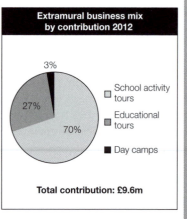

Figure 1.2   **Extramural Ltd: business mix**

In school activity tours Extramural faces a number of competitors who do just that. They are their own independent entities, one or two of which are successful and highly profitable. School activity tours should therefore be treated as a business.

So too for educational tours and day camps, for identical reasons. Extramural's business mix is thus as in Figure 1.2.

School activity tours account for 65% of Extramural's business, but contribute 70% to overheads. Educational tours are the next biggest business, with 32% of sales, but with lower margins they yield only a 27% contribution. Day camps remains a small business but is as profitable as school activity tours, each with 49% contribution margin compared to 41% in educational tours.

Richard and Jane conclude that breakdown into businesses is simple, but do they need to segment any further? Should they, for example, break down their school activity tour business by product/market segment? They investigate further.

Within the school activity tour business, they find distinctive product offerings, sold to distinctive customer segments. Product offerings include pure activity tours, ICT learning combined with activity tours and other combined learning/activity tours – each of which could be further broken down by location of centre, of which there are eight in the UK and two in France. Most different of all are summer residential camps, sold not to school parties but to individuals.

Customer grouping possibilities include Year 6 (aged 10–11) school groups, other year school groups, each perhaps regionally specified, student groups, sports groups and, for summer residential camps, children aged 7–17 grouped perhaps by origin, whether from the UK or other countries, France and the Netherlands in particular. These all seem to be valid customer groups in that they have distinctive customer characteristics and often require different marketing approaches to reach them.

With four to eight major product offerings and five or six customer groups, making potentially around 50 product/market segments, Richard and Jane realise they are in danger of over-complexity. They combine some, redefine others and refine and hone the process until they arrive at just seven major product/market segments for their school activity tours business (see Table 1.1).

Table 1.1	Extramural Ltd: segment mix in school activity tour business		

Extramural's school activity tour business: product/market segments	Share of revenues 2012	2017F
Pure activity tours/Year 6 children	24%	23%
Pure activity tours/other year children	19%	18%
ICT & activity tours/all children	12%	10%
Environment & activity tours/all children	9%	10%
Summer residential camps/UK campers	11%	9%
Summer residential camps/continental campers	14%	15%
Football & activity tours/all children	3%	2%
Language & activity tours/all children [NEW]	2%	6%
Other	6%	7%
Total	**100%**	**100%**

Extramural's main product/market segment in its school activity tour business is pure activity tours for Year 6 children, making up 24% of 2012 revenues. Other main segments contribute fairly evenly, but Richard and Jane are pleased to note that the host of segments other than these seven make up just 8% of revenues.

Next the Davieses turn to the future. Will these same segments be the main drivers of this business in three to five years' time? Might a relatively new segment be developed into a major one? One such could well be language/activity tours, an offering currently selling well where the children combine foreign language learning in the mornings with activities in the afternoons.

They insert an extra column into the table to reflect likely future sales breakdown, plus an extra row for language/activity tours, which they forecast to achieve a 6% share of revenues by 2017. That is significant and they will need to concentrate their research for this business, on markets, competition, competitiveness and so forth, on at least these eight segments.

In their strategy process, the Davieses will need to conduct the analysis segment by segment. Some competitors have offerings in all these segments, with one or two having an even broader offering. One or two players lease sites during the peak school activity tour period and thus offer no summer residential camps.

Certain players are strong in specific segments, less so in others – as for Extramural.

For the purposes of this book, however, such a detailed analysis is not possible – or the central case study would be as lengthy as the whole book. The case study is intended to illustrate the strategy process, not to display an in-depth strategy review of Extramural. We shall therefore be taking Extramural's school activity tours business largely as a single segment for illustrative purposes, likewise Extramural's educational tours and day camps business.

Essential checklist on knowing your business

■ Whether your business is established or starting up, set out which product/market segments matter most in your business mix, now and in the near future.

■ Which contribute, or will contribute, most to sales? To operating profit?

■ Which segments can make or break your business?

2

Setting goals and objectives

8.
CORPORATE
STRATEGY

9. RISK AND ···

··· OPPORTUNITY

7. BUSINESS
STRATEGY

COMPETITIVENESS:

5. CURRENT	6. TARGET

3. MARKET DEMAND	4. INDUSTRY SUPPLY

1. YOUR BUSINESS	2. YOUR AIMS

❝❝ Goals allow you to control the direction of change in your favor.

Brian Tracy

In this chapter

- ▨ Setting long-term goals
- ▨ Setting SMART objectives

You now know your business, but where do you want it to be in three to five years' time? What sort of a firm do you want it to be? On which parameters will you measure performance success?

What are the aims of your firm?

There are numerous treatises written on the relative merits of a company articulating its vision, mission, aims, purposes, goals, objectives, values, principles, ideals, beliefs, principles and so on and so forth. The sound of hair splitting can be deafening.

It is simpler and adequate to stick to two of these: goals and objectives.

A goal is something your business aims to be, as described in words. An objective is a target that helps to measure whether that goal is achieved, and is typically set out in numbers.

One of your goals may be for your business to be the most customer-centric provider of your services in Northern Europe. Objectives to back up that goal could be the achievement of a 'highly satisfied' rating of 30% from your annual customer survey by 2015 and of 35% by 2017, along with 80% 'satisfied' or better by that year.

Goals are directional, objectives are specific. The former should look beyond the short-term and set out where you see the firm in the long term. The latter should be 'SMART', namely Specific, Measurable, Attainable, Relevant and Time-limited – see later in this chapter.

Other aims can readily slot into the simple goals and objectives framework:

- *Mission* – in theory, what sets your business apart from the rest of the competition; in practice, you can treat this as a goal.
- *Vision* – in theory, where your business aims to go or become; again, you can treat this as another goal.
- *Aims* – they can be taken as roughly synonymous with goals.
- *Purposes* – ditto.
- *Values* – in theory, a set of beliefs and principles that guide how your business should respond when there are moral, ethical, safety, health, environmental or other value-related demands on the business that may conflict with the goal of shareholder value maximisation; in practice, this can be identified as a separate goal.
- *Beliefs* – as for values.
- *Ideals* – ditto.
- *Principles* – ditto.

The setting of long-term goals and SMART objectives is essential in strategy development. It is the second of the building blocks in the Strategy Pyramid.

Essential tip

Should your overriding goal be maximising shareholder value? Or should it include corporate social responsibility? Should you strive to achieve an optimal balance between maximising the interests of shareholders with those of other stakeholders, such as employees, customers, the community, the environment?

It is your call. There is an inevitable trade-off. But remember that without shareholder value you have no business. And that would benefit no one – not you, your employees, your customers, not even the taxman – other than your competitors.

Setting long-term goals

Goal setting is the cornerstone of business strategy. Goals should underpin each of your company's main strategic initiatives over the next five years or so.

Goal setting should also prove motivational. Goals can enhance employee performance in four ways, according to Latham and Locke:

- They focus attention towards goal-relevant activities.
- They have an energising effect.
- They encourage persistence.
- They help staff cope with the task at hand.

Here are five considerations when setting goals:

- Goals differ from objectives.
- Short-term goals have little place in strategy development.
- The best goals for motivational purposes may be market related.
- Financial goals may need to resolve the shareholder–stakeholder trade-off.
- Value-related goals are no less valid.

A goal is something your business aims to be, as described in words. An objective is a target that helps to measure whether that goal is achieved, and is typically set out in numbers. Your goal may be to become a low-cost provider in a key segment. An accompanying objective might be to reduce unit operating costs in that segment within three years by 10%.

Secondly, think of short-term goals as what lies within and behind this year's budget. These may be important in the short term, whether for keeping the financial markets or your owners happy or for you to land that performance-related bonus.

But what lies within that budget may have little impact on strategy development. Strategy takes into account market demand trends and industry competition forces that go well beyond the short term. It is no good gearing up your business to compete ferociously in the short term only to be exposed to a drop-off in demand or intensified competition in the medium to long term.

Thirdly, there are various types of goal. Market- or customer-oriented goals are often the most motivational and easy enough to monitor. Market share data is readily collected by companies beyond a certain size. A goal could be market leadership in Segment A within three years. Such a goal is motivational for the salesforce, and often simple to assess progress.

Customer satisfaction or retention goals (or objectives – see the next section) can also have the same effect.

Operational goals are also incentivising for the operations team – and even simpler to monitor than market-related goals. A goal of cost leadership in Segment B within five years can dynamise performance improvement teams. Progress within the company on unit cost reduction can be tracked over time and compared at annual intervals with those of your competitors.

The fourth issue concerns financial goals. If the goals (or objectives) relate to segment prices or margins, whether gross margin or contribution, they can be treated in the same way as market-related goals – motivational for the salesforce, easy to monitor.

But when they relate to the overall financial performance of the company, whether return on sales or capital, the goals may need to resolve a trade-off between maximising shareholder value and balancing the interests of all stakeholders, including employees, customers, suppliers, the environment and the community, not just shareholders.

Finally, your value-related goals may be just as important. One such goal could be an ethical sourcing policy – for example, no child labour used by suppliers or no genetically modified cereals bought in. This is your call, though you will be aware that this may be in conflict with a goal of shareholder value maximisation.

Essential tip

Don't have too many goals. They say people can't remember more than three of any list, but you may choose to stretch that to four or five.

Go for a dozen and you'll be lucky to attain half of them. Go for a handful and you may bag the lot.

Essential example

Life at Mars

What Hoover is to the vacuum cleaner market, so too Mars in choc bars – virtually a generic term.

Yet there is much more to Mars Inc. than its eponymous chocolate bar. It was not even its launch product – that was the Milky Way bar. Many people don't even know that Milky Way belongs to Mars Inc., let alone Maltesers or M&Ms.

Most are also unaware that chocolate confectionery is but one slice of a huge, low-key, private company, with six strategic business units – chocolate, pet care, chewing gum, food, drink and life sciences – despite these units selling such well-known international brands as Pedigree Chum, Wrigley gum and Uncle Ben's rice.

Mars Inc. has revenues of $30 billion and 65,000 employees and has been owned privately by the family since Frank Mars founded it in 1923. His son, Forrest, drove the business forward, personally introducing M&Ms and Uncle Ben's and virtually inventing the pet food industry.

But he was obsessed with secrecy. Fortune magazine honoured him as 'one of this century's most brilliant and successful entrepreneurs', but qualified this with 'an irascible candymaker with a fetish for privacy'. Even upon his death aged 95 in 1999, the company declined to provide details.

The company has since become more open, but there are shades of Forrest in their five core principles of doing business:

- *Quality* – The consumer is our boss, quality is our work, and value for money is our goal.

- *Responsibility* – As individuals, we demand total responsibility from ourselves; as associates, we support the responsibilities of others.

- *Mutuality* – A mutual benefit is a shared benefit; a shared benefit will endure – the actions of Mars should never be at the expense … of others with whom we work.

- *Efficiency* – We use resources to the full, waste nothing and do only what we can do best.

- *Freedom* – We need freedom to shape our future; we need profit to remain free.

Mars Inc. believes that these principles are 'a set of fundamental beliefs that help to shape and define us as a company; they express our vision not only of who we are, but where and what we want to be'.

This is all worthy stuff and perhaps these principles genuinely serve to motivate the Martian employees. But try stating some opposites or antonyms against key words, for example:

- *Quality* – The consumer is our servant.

- *Responsibility* – We demand no responsibility from ourselves.

- *Mutuality* – Our actions should always be at the expense of others.

- *Efficiency* – We waste everything.

- *Freedom* – We need captivity to shape our future.

A company with such principles wouldn't survive too long, implying that those of Mars are self-evident. They represent motherhood and apple pie. Unlike goals and objectives, they seem of little use for purposes of strategy development.

But these principles seem to work for Mars. And there may be lessons for others in this proselytising approach to business.

Setting SMART objectives

Objectives are intimately linked to goals. Your firm aims towards a goal, a destination typically articulated in words. Objectives are targets, whether along the route or at the final destination, and are typically set out in numbers.

You may aim for the goal of UK market leadership in a key segment by 2018. That is a worthy goal, but a bit too vague for a robust strategy. More precise would be the corresponding objectives of attaining 33% market share by 2016 and 35% by 2018. This objective should help deliver your goal of market leadership in that segment.

Where goals are indicative and directional, objectives are precise. You should set objectives that are:

■ *Specific* – A precise number against a particular parameter.

■ *Measurable* – That parameter must be quantifiable, for example a market share percentage in a segment rather than a woolly target such as 'best supplier'.

■ *Attainable* – There is no point in aiming for the improbable – disappointment will be the inevitable outcome.

■ *Relevant* – The objective should relate to the goal; if the goal is market leadership, an objective of winning 'best marketing campaign of the year' in the trade journal would be inappropriate.

■ *Time-limited* – You should specify by when the objective should be achieved; an objective with no time limitation would serve no motivational purpose and result in the slippage of difficult decisions.

Objectives should be *S-M-A-R-T*. The best objectives are indeed smart. As in the example above, the objectives are *Specific* (a market share target in that segment), *Measurable* (market research to which you subscribe will reveal whether the 35% is met), *Attainable* (you are at 29% now and your new product range has been well received), *Relevant* (market share is the ultimate measure of market leadership) and *Time-limited* (2018).

As with goal setting, keep it simple. One or two objectives against each of four or five goals should be fine.

Essential tip

Here is another take on the same theme. Richard Rumelt, in his best-selling book of 2011, *Good Strategy, Bad Strategy*, states that strategy implementation is greatly assisted by the identification of 'proximate objectives'. Each of these is a target that is close enough that the firm 'can reasonably be expected to hit, or even overwhelm it'. He is emphasising the attainable ('A') component of a SMART objective.

He cites the example of President Kennedy pledging to place a man on the moon. The objective sounded fanciful, but it conveyed ambition. And Kennedy had an ace up his sleeve – he knew the technology already existed for such a mission to succeed.

Essential case study

Extramural Ltd Strategic Review, 2013

Chapter 2: Goals and objectives

Richard and Jane Davies's primary aim for their company, specifically for this strategy review process, is to get Extramural into the best possible shape for an exit in five years' time.

But that must not in any way be at the expense of the founding principles of the company, which have remained constant throughout.

At a modest brainstorming session over the dining-room table, accompanied by an excellent bottle of red, the Davieses firm up on three major goals:

- Remain one of the two pre-eminent providers of school activity tours.
- Ensure customer satisfaction, for both teacher and child.
- Maximise shareholder value.

Towards the attainment of these goals, they draw up these six SMART objectives:

- School activity tour market share to rise from 23% to 28% by 2017

■ School rebooking rate to be increased from 66% to 75% by
2015

■ Summer camp occupancy to rise from 62% to 70% by 2015

■ School activity tour contribution margin of 49% to return to
2008's 54% by 2015

■ Educational tour business to improve contribution margin from
41% to 45% by 2015

■ The number of day camps operated to double by 2015 to 12.

Each objective is specific and unambiguous, and is readily
measurable. Each seems achievable – there is nothing
outrageously ambitious about any of them. Each is also relevant
to the company's goals and is time-limited.

In a word, each is SMART.

The Davieses recognise, however, that they may need to revisit
these objectives towards the end of the strategy process. If they
decide to withdraw from one of their three businesses and invest
further in a remaining business, the objectives will need to be
redrawn – but the goals won't change.

Essential checklist on setting goals and objectives

Play with vision, mission, aims, purposes, goals, objectives,
values, principles, ideals, beliefs, principles and their like if you
will, but what matters most for purposes of strategy development
is the setting of long-term goals and *SMART* objectives.

3

Forecasting market demand

> It's better to have the wind at your back than in your face.
>
> *Unattributed*

In this chapter

- Sizing the market
- Forecasting market demand
  - Essential tool: Moving averages

- Forecasting demand for a start-up
- Market demand risks and opportunities

Do you shy away from the word micro-economics? Don't. It lies at the bedrock of strategy, the base of the pyramid. Only once you appreciate the micro-economic context in which your firm operates and with which it interacts will you have the depth of understanding on which to build a robust strategy.

Micro-economics concerns the economic behaviour of individual units of the economy, whether a person, household, firm or industry – as distinct from macro-economics, which deals with the economy as a whole.

There are two distinct but interrelated aspects of micro-economic behaviour to grasp: market demand and industry supply. The latter deals with the forces driving industry competition and their impact on market share, pricing and profitability in your industry, and will be addressed in Chapter 4. This chapter focuses on the former, market demand – how to size it and where it is headed.

Sizing the market

Size is important.

Without market size you may find it hard to gauge market demand growth. And you certainly won't know market share. Without market share, you'll find it hard to judge competitive position. Then you'll find it hard to draw up a winning strategy.

The larger your company, the easier it is to find data on market size. Industry associations proliferate and many either compute market share themselves or contract out the job to specialist market research firms. The latter compete fiercely with each other to cover each and every market where they perceive there to be a sufficient number of customers to turn a profit.

SMEs don't enjoy such lavish attention from market research firms. Some do, and I am often pleasantly surprised when a client turning over £10–20 million reveals monthly market data provided to the firm and its half-dozen competitors by some enterprising market researcher, often a one-man band.

Most SMEs don't. And they are not alone. A medium-sized firm turning over £100 million may well have the bulk of its business covered by market research reports, but not necessarily that star business segment turning over £10 million, with only two main competitors and growing at 15% per year. That segment may as yet be too small with too few potential customers to entice a market researcher.

Where no data on market size can be found off the shelf, you have to size the market yourself.

First you must decide what you are looking for: your addressed market or your addressable market. The difference can be huge:

■ *Addressed market* – those to whom you currently offer your goods or services and who may or may not purchase them.

■ *Addressable (or available) market* – all those whom you *could* serve should you extend your offering.

There are six main ways of sizing a market:

■ *Top-down market research*. Start with a known, researched market size and chop out inapplicable sections, or make appropriate assumptions on relevant proportions, to drill down to the target market.

■ *Bottom-up market research*. Take disaggregated data from a market research report and assemble the relevant bits that make up your target market.

■ *Bottom-up customer sizing*. Estimate how much each major customer spends in this target market and make an allowance for other, minor customers.

■ *Bottom-up competitor sizing (or 'marketcrafting': see below)*. Estimate the scale of your competitors in the target market.

■ *Related market triangulation*. Use two, three or more known sizes of related markets to gauge a rough estimate of the target market.

■ *Final triangulation*. Juggle the estimates from the above sources and subject them to sanity checks. Why the differences? Which method do you feel most confident with; on balance, what *feels* right? Consider giving each estimate a reliability rating, work out relative probabilities and compute a weighted average estimate of target market size.

Marketcrafting is a particularly useful method, since it gives you the base data needed not just for market demand analysis (this chapter) but for industry supply too (next chapter). It is a technique I developed some years ago for clients who knew their customers and competitors well enough but had no firm grasp on market scale. I have used it primarily in niche markets, or in segments of larger markets, but now and again in larger markets too. I recently used it to estimate a market size of around £175 million in an engineering segment left curiously unattended by market research groups.

There are seven main steps in marketcrafting:

1 Select your main competitors – those you pitch regularly against, those you exhibit alongside at trade shows – and don't forget the foreign competitors, especially those from lower-cost countries.

2 Take competitor A: do you think they are selling more or less than you into this market? If less, by how much less, *very roughly*? Are they selling half as much as you? Three-quarters? If they sell more than you, by how much more, very roughly? 10% more? A third more? Is there any publicly available information which can guide you on this? (Competitor A's sales to this market are unlikely to be available if it is a private company, but employment data can be indicative. What do customers tell you? And suppliers?)

3 Taking your current sales level as an index number of 100, assign the appropriate index number to competitor A. If you think they sell less than you in this market, but not that much less, say 10% less, give them an index number of 90.

4 Repeat steps 2 and 3 for each of the competitors named in step 1.

5 Make an allowance for any other competitors you have not named, those who are small or those who only appear now and again; this should also be an index number. If you think all these others together sell about half what you sell to the market, give this 'Others' category an index number of 50.

6 Add up all the index numbers, divide the total by 100 and multiply by your level of sales – that is your preliminary estimate of market size.

7 Ask your sales director to do the same exercise; get her to talk to the guy in the sales team who used to work at competitor A and the woman in R&D whose former boyfriend now works at competitor B. Get their inputs, and those of your operations director and head of R&D; where their views differ from yours, discuss and refine the numbers. You have now built a reasoned estimate of market size.

Marketcrafting is hardly an accurate process, nor can it be guaranteed that the final number will not be some way out. But it is better than nothing, very much better, because you can now use the results to get values of three parameters key to strategy development:

■ *Market growth*. Repeat the marketcrafting exercise above to estimate the market size of three years ago. For example, did competitor A sell more or less than you to this market three years ago, before that new plant came into operation, and by how much? And so on. You now have two data points – the market size of today and that of three years ago. Punch them into your calculator and out will come an average compound growth rate over the three years, an estimate of recent market growth.

■ *Market share.* Now you 'know' the market size, you also know your market share (your sales level divided by the estimated market size); you also have an estimate of the market share of each of your competitors.

■ Best of all, *market share change.* You now have your market share of three years ago, as well as that of today, so you have an estimate of your market share gain (or loss), as well as that of each of your competitors. These estimates will be most useful in assessing both competitive intensity (Chapter 4) and relative competitive position (Chapter 5).

Table 3.1 shows an example of the findings that can be deduced from the process, adapted from the engineering company I worked with referred to above.

Table 3.1   **Marketcrafting: an example**

Competitor	Estimated index number for sales (latest year)	Implied market share (%)
The Company	= 100	17%
Competitor A	120	21%
Competitor B	85	15%
Competitor Group C	125	21%
Competitor Group D	65	11%
Competitor E	30	5%
Competitor F	20	3%
Others	40	7%
Total	**585**	**100%**

The company's turnover in this segment was about £30 million, so the market size could be estimated at 585 ÷ 100 × 30, or around £175 million. The company's market share emerged at 17% (100/585), rather lower than the 25% management had quoted prior to the marketcrafting exercise. Likewise, the market share of the Far Eastern competitors, group C, though significant at 21%, did not seem to be as high as the one-third quoted rather sensationally in the trade press.

When we repeated the exercise to estimate market size of three years earlier, we found that the market had contracted heavily during the post-credit crunch recession, falling by one-third, or by roughly 10% per year. Meanwhile Far Eastern competitors had grown share greatly from 9% to 21%, with corresponding share losses by the domestic players, including that of the company, from 20% to 17%.

These were important findings. The trends were of course known beforehand, but their quantification through the marketcrafting method, though very rough, put some of the wilder assertions into perspective and helped focus attention on the strategic challenge ahead.

Essential tip

Treat the results with caution. If your marketcrafting suggests a competitor's market share of 25% and you hear that their sales director has been boasting of 30–35% share at a recent trade show, don't dismiss it offhand as sales spiel. Take another look at your numbers. Is there any way the competitor may be right? Do they have access to information that you don't? What would that imply for your share, or other competitors' shares?

The numbers are rough, very rough. But they are better than nothing and seldom misleading. And they will come in very handy in Chapters 4 and 5.

Forecasting market demand

The quote at the beginning of this chapter, about it being better to have the wind at your back than in your face, is one that is often heard in the business world.

It's a question of odds. You have a better chance of prospering in a market that's growing than in one that's shrinking.

Market size is all very well, but what often matters more in strategy development is what the market is doing, where it is going – the dynamics, as opposed to the statics. Is market demand in your main business segments growing, shrinking or flat-lining?

This is the big question. It's not the only one, of course. Equally important, as we'll see in the next couple of chapters, is the nature of the competition you face and how you're placed to compete. But it's the first big question.

I developed many years ago a four-step process for translating market demand trends and drivers into forecasts. I call it the HOOF approach, for two reasons. HDDF, the strict representation of the first letters in each of the four steps, would be an unattractive, unmemorable acronym – but, with the appropriate creative licence, the circular O can be borrowed as a lookalike to the semi-circular D!

And also because it reminds me fondly of the youth football team I coach. No matter how many times I screech at a couple of players to play the simple ball out of defence, head up, along the ground, to a nearby player, they blindly HOOF it down the pitch with all their might, as far as their adolescent muscles can propel it!

As the ball leaves the foot, the HOOF starts the perfect trajectory of growth – the kind of market demand forecast we would all love for our business (before the ball reaches its summit and plummets to the ground, the standard path of the product life cycle – Chapter 6).

There are four distinct stages in the HOOF approach to demand forecasting. Get this process right and all falls logically into place. Get it out of step and you may end up with a misleading answer. You need to apply these steps for each of your main business segments.

The four steps are:

1 *Historic growth* – Assess how market demand has grown in the past.
2 *Drivers past* – Identify what has been driving that past growth.
3 *Drivers future* – Assess whether there will be any change in influence of these and other drivers in the future.
4 *Forecast growth* – Forecast market demand growth, based on the influence of future drivers.

Let's look at each of these briefly, then at some examples.

1. Historic growth. This is where you need to get some facts and figures. If you have access to market research data, whether on a regular basis or with a one-off purchase, all your needs should be in there. If not, you may have to do some marketcrafting – see the previous tool.

Be careful not to fall into the trap of relying on one recent number.

Just because demand for a service jumped by, say, 8% last year doesn't mean that trend growth in that market has been 8% per year. The latest year may have been an aberration. The market may have dipped two years ago, remained static last year and recovered by 8% this year. Average annual growth over the three years might have been only 2% per year.

You should try to get an average annual (compound) growth rate over a number of recent years, preferably the last three or four. As long as there haven't been serious annual ups and downs, and there may well have been in the period 2008–11, you can usually get a usable approximation of average annual growth by calculating the overall percentage change in, say, the last four years and then annualising it. If there have been ups and downs, you should smooth them out with three-year moving averages before calculating the percentage change – see the essential tool text box.

Essential tool

Moving averages

Where markets have been up and down, showing no consistent trend, take care with the H step of the HOOF approach to demand forecasting.

The best way to deal with market volatility is to plot a graph on logarithmic paper and draw a line of best fit through the points.

But you may not be comfortable with graphs, especially those of the logarithmic variety. A simple, non-graphical alternative is to translate the data into moving averages. This enables annual fluctuations to be smoothed out, making it easier to decipher and calculate trend growth rates.

Take the set of market data and apply these steps:

- Observe the length of the cycle and select an appropriate time period for smoothing, often a three-year period.
- Take the annual average of values during that time period around any given year (if the cycle is three years, take an average of values for the given year, the previous year and the succeeding year).
- Calculate compound growth rates between appropriate start and end points to establish the trend.

The example in Table 3.2 may help, taken directly from a job I did a few years ago.

Table 3.2 **Smoothing with moving averages: an example**

	2000	2001	2002	2003	2004	2005	2006	2007
Actual demand (£m)	1426	1223	1150	1201	1387	1452	1582	1555
Actual change/ year (%)	n/a	−17%	−6%	4%	15%	5%	9%	−2%
Smoothed demand (£m)	**n/a**	**1283**	**1191**	**1246**	**1347**	**1474**	**1530**	**n/a**
Implied change/ year (%)	n/a	n/a	−7%	5%	8%	9%	4%	n/a

If we were to ignore all that happened in the middle years of this period, and just consider growth between the start point of 2000 and the end point of 2007, that would give an overall increase of 5.4%, or growth (compound) of 0.75% per year.

But 2000 was the peak of the dotcom boom, so using that as the base year would underestimate trend growth in the 2000s. Likewise, if we'd used the trough year 2002 as the base, that would have produced an overestimate. We therefore translate the above data into three-year moving averages – namely the sum of each year's number plus the previous year's number plus the following year's number, divided by 3.

This has the effect of smoothing the annual fluctuations and we begin to see a clearer pattern. Taking 2001 as the start point and 2006 as the end point now gives an overall increase of 19%, or an average of 3.6% per year (over five smoothed years, not seven actual years). The one decimal point suggests spurious accuracy, but a conclusion of 3.5% per year, plus or minus 0.5% per year (or, in other words, 3–4% per year), seemed reflective of trend growth in the 2000s in this market.

But don't just compute the numbers blindly. Try to understand what has been happening in each of the years to produce such irregular numbers. That will help you avoid the trap of selecting a boom (or bust) year as the starting point and a bust (or boom) year as the end point. Taking boom to boom, bust to bust, average to average periods should give similar answers, but mixing them up can be severely misleading (and is a much-loved ruse of the politician!).

One word of caution: market demand growth is generally measured, analysed and forecast in real terms. You should take care to understand the differences between these growth rates:

- In nominal terms, that is with goods (or services) priced in the money of the day.
- In real terms, which is the growth rate in nominal prices deflated by the growth rate in the average prices of goods in that market; this growth rate, as long as the correct deflators are used, should be a measure of volume growth.

You should be consistent and restrict all analysis of comparative market growth rates to those in real terms in this chapter and throughout the strategy development process.

But should you need to proceed to business planning and financial forecasting, you must bring average price forecasts back into the mix. Then your revenue forecasts, as well as the whole P&L, will be directly comparable with market growth rate forecasts in nominal prices.

2. Drivers past. Once you have uncovered some information on recent market demand growth, find out what has been influencing that growth. Typical factors that influence demand in many markets are:

- Per capita income growth
- Population growth in general
- Population growth specific to a market (for example, of pensioners or baby boomers, or general population growth in a particular area)
- Some aspect of government policy or purchasing
- Changing awareness, perhaps from high levels of promotion by competing providers
- Business structural shifts (such as towards outsourcing)
- Price change
- Fashion, even a craze

■ Weather – seasonal variations, but maybe even the longer-term effects of climate change.

Or your sector may be heavily influenced by demand in other sectors, typically customer sectors. Thus the demand for steel is heavily dependent on demand for automobiles, ships, capital goods equipment and construction. Demand for automobiles is also the major driver for demand for Tier 1 car seat suppliers, which in turn drives demand for Tier 2 steel seat reclining mechanism suppliers, who in turn buy from specialist steel producers.

A vertical sector relationship may be so close that you may be able to obtain sound estimates of derived demand. You can obtain excellent automotive market forecasts from specialist market research companies, thereby guiding Tier 2 suppliers like seat mechanism producers in their forecasts.

But be careful of derived demand forecasts – there are always *other* drivers. The average number of seats per car sold may be changing due to the popularity of 4 × 4s. A major car company may decide to opt for an alternative car seat technology.

The same applies in deriving demand forecasts from those in comple-mentary or related sectors. Thus demand growth for accommodation in three-star hotels in the West Country will be influenced by demand growth for coach package tours, but it will not be the same. The latter will not be the only driver of the former. Another driver is the sterling–euro exchange rate, which will be a major influence on whether cost-conscious coach travellers from the North of England opt for destinations in the West Country, France or further afield.

3. Drivers future. Now you need to assess how each of these drivers is likely to develop over the next few years. Are things going to carry on more or less as before for a driver? Or are things going to change significantly?

Will, for instance, immigration continue to drive local population growth? Is the government likely to hike up a local tax? Could this market become less fashionable?

What are the prospects for growth in vertical or complementary sectors?

The most important driver is, of course, the economic cycle. If it seems the economy is poised for a nosedive, that could have a serious impact on demand in your business over the next year or two – assuming your business is relatively sensitive (or 'elastic', in economics-speak) to the economic cycle. Or maybe your business is relatively inelastic, as, for example, in much of the food industry? You may need to think carefully about the timing of the economic cycle and the elasticity of your business.

4. Forecast growth. This is the fun bit. You've assembled all the information on past trends and drivers. Now you can weave it all together, sprinkle it with a large dose of judgement, and you have a forecast of market demand – not without risk, not without uncertainty, but a systematically derived forecast nevertheless.

Let's take a simple example of the HOOF approach in action. In one of your business segments, your firm offers a relatively new service to the elderly. Step 1 **(H)**: You find that the market has been growing at 5–10% per year over the last few years. Step 2 **(O)**: You identify the main drivers as (a) per capita income growth, (b) growth in the elderly population, and (c) growing awareness of the service by elderly people. Step 3 **(O)**: You believe that income growth will continue as before, the elderly population will grow even faster in the future, and awareness can only get more widespread. Step 4 **(F)**: You conclude that growth in your market will accelerate and could reach over 10% per year over the next few years.

The HOOF approach is best used diagrammatically. The example above is simple, but it becomes even simpler when displayed on a diagram

Table 3.3 The HOOF approach to demand forecasting: an example

Demand drivers for a new service to the elderly	Impact on demand growth			Comments
	Recent past	Now	Next few years	
Growth in incomes	–	0	+	· US to resume economic growth 2012–13, assuming no double-dip
Growth in elderly population	+	+	++	· Proportion of US population aged 65+ forecast to grow from 13% to 18.5% by 2025 (US Census Bureau)
Increased awareness of service	++	++	+++	· Newspaper coverage, national and local, greater all the time
Overall impact	+	+	++	
Market growth rate	5 to 10%/yr	5 to 10%	Over 10%/yr	
	H	O	O	F

Key to driver impact

+++	Very strong positive
++	Strong positive
+	Some positive
0	None
–	Some negative
– –	Strong negative
– – –	Very strong negative

– see Table 3.3. The impact of each demand driver on demand growth is represented by varying numbers of plus and minus signs, or a zero. In this case you can see that there will be more pluses in the near future than there were in the past, implying that demand growth will accelerate – from the historic 5–10% per year to the future 10+% per year.

In real-world strategy development, there will be more such charts, one for each key product/market segment, and each will have more drivers. But the fundamental principles of the HOOF approach will remain. The chart will show the historic growth rate (H), identify the relative impact of drivers past and future (O & O) and conclude with a growth forecast for that segment (F).

And now for an example of how not to do it. Many years ago I was doing some work for a crane manufacturer in the North of England and came across a draft business plan. In the section on market demand, its young author had stated there was no data on UK demand for cranes to be found anywhere. So, for the purposes of the financial forecasts, he assessed real growth in the crane market to be the same as for UK engineering output as a whole, forecast then by OECD at 2.4% per year.

Oops! The mistake was one of exclusion. Yes, macro-economic demand was an important driver of demand in the crane market, as for all engineering output. But there were three or four other drivers of as great importance, on which there was, admittedly, no hard and fast data but plenty of anecdotal evidence. They included evidence of crane destocking, a thriving second-hand market and, above all, an imminent downturn in high-rise construction activity.

None of these drivers bore any relation to engineering output as a whole, and their combined impact served to translate a 2.4% per year crane market growth forecast into one of steep decline, possibly at 10% per year for two or three years.

The moral of the tale is to make sure *all* drivers are taken into account, *irrespective of whether hard data can be found on them*. The HOOF process encourages you to seek out all relevant drivers and assess their influence in a structured, combined quantitative and qualitative context, using balanced judgement where required.

Essential example

No wrap for the cinema

In the mid-1980s, I was tasked to do a quick review of a business plan for a company intent on opening a string of multiplex cinemas in Britain. The concept had taken off in the US. Would it work in the UK?

Cinema attendance in the days before television had been an integral part of the British way of life. Numbers peaked at 1.64 billion in post-war 1946 – equivalent to 33 visits to the cinema that year by every man, woman *and child* in the UK! That is one visit every eight or nine days by every single person in the country.

Television changed all that, offering moving picture entertainment from the comfort of the living room. Cinema attendance went on a prolonged downward trend as more and more households acquired the televiewing habit. By the 1980s video ownership and rental had accelerated the decline and the end seemed in sight for the cinema.

By 1984 UK cinema attendances had dropped to 54 million, not much bigger than the 35 million who went to see one film alone, *Gone with the Wind*, in the UK in the 1940s. It had dropped like a stone from 100 million in 1980.

And yet there seemed to be some sort of recovery going on. In 1985 attendances had bounced back to 70 million and in 1986 had consolidated at 73 million. It was 1987 when I looked at this business plan. What was going on? Could the UK cinema industry be reborn?

There were two demand drivers that seemed particularly promising:

- *The advent of multiplexes* – the first such, the Point in Milton Keynes, with 10 screens, had sold 2 million tickets in its first two years and its bustling foyer had become a social meeting point for the youth of the city.

- *The upgrading of former 'flea pits'* – with consumers in London and other cities seemingly prepared to pay a bit more for a more comfortable and uplifting experience.

But the demand risks remained huge, including the following possibilities:

■ Milton Keynes may not be representative of the country as a whole.

■ Mutliplexes, if successful, may put small single-screen cinemas out of business, leaving minimal net gain.

■ Multiplexes may be a fad.

■ DVDs were taking over from video cassettes, raising the prospect of improved quality home movie experience.

■ All the socio-economic factors behind the prolonged downward trend in cinema attendances since the 1940s remained.

On balance, it seemed worth the punt. Multiplexes seemed a ray of sunshine. Cinema attendances appeared more likely to maintain their recovery, rather than slip back into decline. But my colleagues were more risk-averse and our bank withdrew from the deal.

A bad call. Cinema attendances carried on rising and by 1990 had recovered to the 100 million level of 10 years earlier. And they did not stop there – they carried on growing, with the occasional annual blip, at an average 2.5 to 3.0% per year right through to today, reaching around 175 million in 2012.

Britons now go to the cinema on average three times a year – way, way down on the 1940s, but not too far below the US at four times and, keenest of all, Iceland at five times.

And what of the future? Positive demand drivers now include luxury cinemas, 3D films and the occasional blockbuster, like a new James Bond film or one with a DC or Marvel character. Offset against this are excellent quality large-screen televisions, also with 3D.

Another negative driver is competition not just from television, video, Internet and computer games, but also the likes of LOVEFiLM, not far distant from the industry's ultimate goal of video-on-demand.

Then there is the improved quality of drama on television, whether it be Sherlock, Homeland or Borgen. With playback capabilities such as iPlayer and personal video recorders, let alone DVD box sets, viewers can accumulate so much must-watch past television that they can never find the time to view it all – let alone go to the cinema.

Finally, the film industry faces the challenge of finding another franchise to rival the extraordinary success of the Harry Potter and Lord of the Rings series.

It is a tough call. But one thing is for sure – cinemas will not go with the wind.

Forecasting demand for a start-up

This building block of the Strategy Pyramid is perhaps the trickiest of all in a start-up. Yours may be a new product or service designed to convey a customer benefit not previously realisable.

In which case, how do you define the market? What is market demand for a product that has not previously existed? What is its size? What are its growth prospects?

On the other hand, your start-up may be in a market that's already well defined – like a guest house, which may well be unique and distinctive, but fits snugly into an already buoyant market for three- to four-star tourism in your region.

Or you may be opening a boutique selling designer childrenswear on the High Street. Again that is a definable, existing market, to be researched in the same way as set out above.

But what if yours is indeed something that has not existed before? How can you convince your backer that there will be buyers of your product or service, and at that price? You need evidence.

You'll have to do some test marketing. If yours is a business-to-business proposition, get on the phone and set up meetings with prospective corporate buyers. Explain the benefits of your product and why at that price they have a bargain.

Keep a record of these meetings and analyse the findings. Write a report drawing out key conclusions from the discussions, with each supported by bulleted evidence – whether comments from named customers, comments from third parties quoted in the press, or data dug up off the web. Collate them into a short and sharp market research report, which will be an appendix to your strategy document.

If yours is a business-to-consumer product or service, test it on the High Street. Get out your clipboard, stand outside an Asda or a Waitrose, depending on your target customer, and talk to people. If you're offering a product, show them. If a service, explain its benefits lucidly but swiftly.

Again, collate the responses, analyse them, draw firm conclusions, support them with quotes and data, and stick the market research report in your appendix.

Now, based on those responses, make an estimate of your potential market size. Imagine there are many suppliers of your product or service and that the whole country is aware of its existence, what would the market size be? How does that compare with the market size for products or services not a million miles different from what you'll be offering? Does your estimate make sense?

And how about market demand growth? If your start-up is serving an existing market, then you can use the same four-stage process for demand forecasting that an established business would use.

If your start-up is for a new market, you may try the same four-stage process, but your primary concern should be the existence of such a market in the first place. Any growth on top of discovering and serving a new market will be icing on the cake.

Essential tip

If your business is a start-up, test the market. Pick up the phone or get out and talk to people. Do some primary market research. Amass, digest and analyse pertinent data. Be armed for the inevitable grilling from your backer.

Market demand risks and opportunities

You have now come to a reasonable forecast of what's likely to happen to market demand in your key business segments over the next few years. But what are the risks of something happening to market demand that could make things worse than that? What could make things much worse? How likely are these risks to happen?

On the other hand, what could make things better than you have forecast? Or much better? How likely are these opportunities to happen?

You need to think carefully about these risks and opportunities. Come Chapter 8, you'll be weighing up all the risks and opportunities around your business strategy. And market demand issues will be the first set to be factored in.

Identify the main half-dozen risks that might affect your market demand forecasts and assess them from two perspectives:

- How likely are they to take place – low, medium or high likelihood?
- If they do occur, how big an impact will they have – low, medium or large impact?

Now do the same for the opportunities identified.

Are any of these risks or opportunities 'big' issues? We'll define a 'big' risk or opportunity as one where:

- The likelihood of occurrence is medium (or high) and the impact is high, or
- The likelihood of occurrence is high and the impact is medium (or high).

Any big issues of market demand need to be flagged clearly in your strategy development process. If it is a big risk, you must consider how you are going to address it and mitigate its impact. If it is a big opportunity, you must consider how to exploit it.

As so often, a table or chart helps clarify the thinking – see the example for Extramural Ltd, Table 3.5, below.

Essential case study

Extramural Ltd Strategic Review, 2013

Chapter 3: Market demand

Richard and Jane Davies have been in the school activity tour business for over 20 years. They have seen some ups and downs in market demand, but on the whole understand and are thankful that they have been working in a reasonably resilient industry.

Like many entrepreneurs and managers who have been in a business for a good while, they think they know the answers to market demand forecasts – in this case, slow and steady. But, out of respect for this guidebook, they decide to follow the HOOF approach step by step and see what emerges.

Table 3.4 Extramural Ltd: market demand for school activity tours

Demand drivers	Impact on demand growth			
UK school activity tour market (commercial providers)	Recent past	Now	Next few years	Comments
Growth in incomes	–/0	0	+	• OECD forecasts 2013–15 real PDI recovery
Growth in school population	0/+	0/+	+	• Primary school bulge to affect Year 6 in 2016–20?
Government encouragement	0/+	0/+	0/+	• Cross-party support continues
Teacher union backing	0/+	0/+	0/+	• One union against, others in favour
LEA Centre investment	–	0	0	• Many centres now refitted, often from Lottery funds
LEA Centre closures	+	0/+	0	• Those remaining often to good scale and standard
Peak demand approaching?	0	0	0	• Only half of primary schools use a commerical provider
Child serious injury	0	0	0	• The risk remains – see Table 3.3
Overall impact	0/+	0/+	+	
Growth rates (% p. a.)				
Market volume	0.5	1	1–2	• Pricing can leverage
Pricing	1	1.5	2	excess demand in
Nominal market value	1.5	2.5	3–4	peak season

First they identify the main demand drivers, including macro-economic factors, school population, Government and trade union support and the future of local government-owned centres – direct competitors to commercial providers in that they compete for the same children's time and wallet during the same period, even though their offerings differ. They assess how these drivers have been influencing demand growth in recent years and how their influence is likely to change in the near future.

Their main findings are:

- ▨ Real personal disposable income is forecast to pick up modestly over the next few years, following its contraction in 2009–11.
- ▨ The bulge in primary school admissions caused by large-scale immigration to the UK in the 2000s will work through to Year 6 from 2016.
- ▨ Support for school activity tours during term time from both Government and teacher unions can be expected to continue.
- ▨ Former demand growth created by the closure of centres owned by local education authorities will diminish, given that the remaining stock is now mainly well invested and viable.

Weighing up these and other demand drivers, the Davieses forecast that demand growth for school activity tours should rise from 0.5% per year in recent years (in real terms) to 1–2% per year over the next few years (see Table 3.4).

That is more or less what the Davieses would have come up with if they had used just their judgement, rather than the HOOF approach. It is only when they move on to the next step that they see the real merit of the approach.

Strategy development is not just about making best judgements in each block of the Strategy Pyramid. It is about assessing the risk and opportunity around those judgements.

They look again at the demand drivers. What if one or more do not turn out to influence demand as expected? What if the unexpected happens and has an adverse impact on demand? Just how adverse could that impact be?

Richard and Jane are not too concerned at the threat of triple-dip recession – they have lived with the double dip, taken the hit on margins, tightened belts and survived.

Table 3.5   **Extramural Ltd: market risk in school activity tours**

Market demand risks	Likelihood	Impact	Comments
Triple-dip recession	L/M	Low	• The industry has weathered the double-dip recession post-2008 crash reasonably well
Government policy U-turn	Low	High	• Cross-party support for outdoor, residential experience for schoolchildren during term-time over last ten years
Union concerns	Low	Med	• Little impact to date of one union's concerns on teacher responsibility for child safety
Child serious injury	Low	High	• No serious injury at an AALA centre *on licensed activities* since formation, let alone through negligence

Market demand opportunities	Likelihood	Impact	Comments
Union changes stance	L/M	Med	• Dogmatic anti stance, but dissenting voices within
Further LEA Centre closures	Low	L/M	• Many remaining centres have good, well invested facilities
Government promotional schemes	Low	Med	• Social engineering expensive in austere times

But what if Government were to withdraw support for school activity tours during term time? Unlikely, perhaps, since all three main political parties are vociferously in favour of such character-building development. But, with so much pressure on meeting educational targets, the possibility of a more conservative voice triumphing exists. Government withdrew support for school ski tours during term time with the introduction of the National Curriculum in 1988, whereupon the market for school ski trips dropped by three-quarters. Could this happen too to school activity tours?

And what of teacher union support? One large union has long discouraged its members from joining school activity tours, whether to LEA or commercial providers, claiming that teachers cannot be guaranteed exemption from personal responsibility for child safety. There are voices in the other teacher unions which advocate likewise.

And what of child safety itself? Following the tragic events at a boating incident in Lyme Bay in 1992, the industry has been transformed and overseen by both an industry association and a regulatory body. Accidents have occurred, but no child has since died at a licensed centre while engaged in licensed activities – a record the industry is proud of and desperate to maintain. But what if the unlikely were to occur?

The Davieses realise that the very existence of their business is subject to an unusually extreme degree of risk. Market demand could be hugely impacted by adverse change in any one of three major risks – Government U-turn, union U-turn, child serious injury. Low probability, yes, but with a huge impact on market demand (see Table 3.5).

There are counterbalancing opportunities – Government might resuscitate some of the schemes for subsidising developmental trips for children from inner-city schools it ran in the mid-2000s, or the one teacher union opposing school activity tours might come in line with the others.

But the Davieses know that their emergent strategy, to be developed in line with expected slow growth in market demand, must be cognisant of the great risks faced by the whole industry. Extramural must play its full part in mitigating those risks, perhaps through taking leadership in the industry association to promote the benefits of the product to Government, teacher unions and parents and in ensuring, in association with the regulator, that child safety remains paramount and at the core of every decision made in the further development of the industry.

Essential checklist on forecasting market demand

Set out for each of your main business segments, succinctly but convincingly, your assessments of:

- Market size – find a source or perhaps craft it yourself
- Market demand growth in recent years – likewise
- Demand drivers and how these are changing
- Forecasts of future market demand – based on future demand drivers
- Market demand risks and opportunities.

If your business is a start-up in a new market niche, concentrate in Chapter 3 on the rationale for the very existence of that niche. Undertake primary market research to unearth evidence to justify that niche.

4

Gauging industry competition

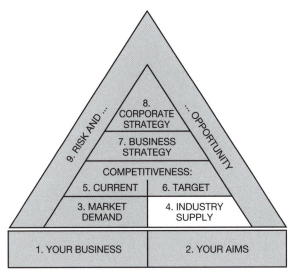

❝ The trouble with the rat race is that even if you win you are still a rat.

Lily Tomlin

In this chapter

- Assessing competitive intensity
- Assigning customer purchasing criteria
- Deriving key success factors
  - Essential tool: Economies of scale

▓ Gauging competition in a start-up

▓ Industry competition risks and opportunities

Face it. You are not alone. There are others who offer the same, or very similar, products or services as you.

They are your competition. Pay them due respect. Then outwit them.

But first think about the issues that apply to all of you, to you and to them. These are the issues of industry competition.

This is the other twin aspect of micro-economics that you need to grasp. The first was market demand, covered in the last chapter. Market demand and industry competition, demand and supply, together compose the micro-economy in which your firm operates.

This chapter also includes two essential tools which could arguably form their own building block, namely assessing customer purchasing criteria ('CPCs') and deriving key success factors ('KSFs'). They form the basic analysis upon which the study of competitiveness in Chapters 5 and 6 can build.

Assessing competitive intensity

Michael Porter's five forces analysis is the pre-eminent tool in this building block and has been since the early 1980s.

It remains the *sine qua non* of micro-economic analysis for business strategy. Porter was himself an industry economist and much of his work was effectively a reinterpretation of established micro-economic theory.

His genius has been in taking some quite difficult economic concepts and presenting them in an everyman way, with a diagrammatic representation and sets of checklists accessible not just to fellow economists but to every manager.

His basic premise is this: competitive intensity determines industry profitability. To determine the latter, you must first understand the former. And there are five fundamental forces which drive competitive intensity (see Figure 4.1):

▓ Internal rivalry

▓ Threat of new entrants

▓ Ease of substitution

▓ Customer power

▓ Supplier power.

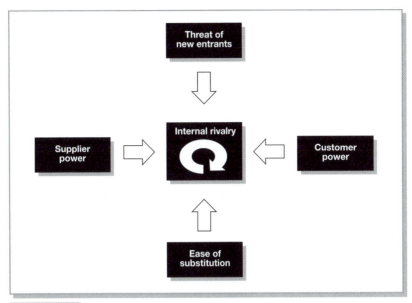

Figure 4.1 **Five forces shaping competition**

Source: Adapted from Porter, M.E., *Competitive Strategy: Techniques for Analyzing Industries and Competitors* (The Free Press, 2004)

Each of the five forces will be examined briefly below.

Internal rivalry

Internal rivalry is shaped by three main sub-forces: the number of players, market demand growth relative to supply, and external pressures.

■ *The number of players.* The more numerous the players, the tougher typically the competition.

■ *Market demand growth.* The slower-growing the market, the tougher typically the competition.

And what of supply? Are demand and supply in balance? Where there is balance, internal rivalry may well be moderate. Where there is oversupply – where supply exceeds demand – internal rivalry will be intensified, and a dampener will be placed on prices. Conversely, where there is undersupply (or excess demand), where customers compete for relatively scarce supplies, internal rivalry will be modest – and you and your competitors may be able to nudge up pricing above inflation.

■ *External pressures.* External bodies, in particular government and the trade unions, have great power to influence the nature of competition in many industries. Government regulation, taxation and subsidies can skew both market demand and the competitive landscape. Trade unions can influence competition in a number of ways, for example through restrictive practices which serve to raise barriers to entry.

There are other, perhaps lesser factors influencing internal rivalry. Barriers to exit are one such. Where providers have little choice but to stay on competing when they should be withdrawing (for example, a restaurant with many employees, hence potentially high redundancy costs, or a service business with a long lease on office space which is difficult to offload), competition is intensified. Low barriers to exit, such as in the minicab business, reduce internal rivalry. Seasonal or irregular overcapacity is another factor. Fluctuating levels of demand (for example, in the fruit picking or ice cream industries) intensify competition.

Threat of new entrants

The lower the barriers to entry to a market, the tougher typically the competition. Barriers to entry can be related to technology, operations, people or cost, where a new entrant has to:

- Develop or acquire a certain technology
- Develop or acquire a certain operational process
- Gain access to a limited distribution channel
- Train or engage scarce personnel
- Invest heavily in either capital assets or marketing to become a credible provider.

Switching costs also influence entry barriers. The higher the costs to the customer of switching from one supplier to another, the higher are the entry barriers. A drinks manufacturer may shift from one sugar supplier to another with relative ease, but may require redesign of the factory in switching from one labelling solution to another.

Ease of substitution

The easier it is for customers to use a substitute product or service, the tougher typically the competition.

Consider the impact of the likes of iTunes in the music industry. It was a substitute solution to the sale of CDs in the high street and a contributory factor, along with e-commerce and the supermarkets, to the demise of retailers such as Woolworths and Zavvi.

Customer power

The more bargaining power customers possess, the tougher typically the competition. Ask any supplier to the supermarket chains, or to automotive manufacturers.

Often this is no more than a reflection of the number of providers in a marketplace, compared with the number of customers. The more choice of provider the customer has, the tougher the competition.

Customer power is also influenced by switching costs. If it's easy and relatively painless to switch supplier, competition is tougher. If switching costs are high, competition diminishes.

Supplier power

The more bargaining power suppliers possess, the tougher typically the competition.

Again it can be just a function of numbers. There are, for example, numerous steel or aluminium converters, but few (and increasingly fewer) metal producers. When metal converters sell components to automotive manufacturers, they can find themselves in a vice-like squeeze with huge steel or aluminium suppliers at one end, and auto giant customers at the other. But the best of them learn how to duck, dive and survive.

Overall competitive intensity

These are the five main forces shaping the degree of competition in a marketplace. Put them all together, and you'll have a measure of how competitive your industry is.

In some industries, such as soft drinks, software and toiletries, all five forces operate benignly to boost profitability – and consistently over the decades. In other industries, like the airlines or textiles, the opposite is true – all five forces act against the airlines and average profitability over the years is dreadful.

How tough is internal rivalry in your industry? And the threat of new entrants or substitutes? How much power do customers and suppliers have on you and your competitors? In short, how intense is competition in your industry? High, low, medium? Or somewhere in between?

And what of the future? Is industry competition set to intensify? Because however tough it is at the moment, it results in you and your competitors getting an average operating margin of a certain per cent.

But will competitive forces conspire to threaten that margin over the next few years? Or has the industry competition of the last few years been unsustainable and likely to ease off in the future?

In short, what will be the effect of competitive dynamics on pricing in your industry over the next few years?

Will competition intensify and put pressure on prices? Will it stay more or less as it is, with pricing moving as it has been doing in recent times? Or will competition ease off, enabling players to nudge up pricing over the next few years?

Essential tip

Porter's model has had its critics over the years. Some believe that boundary definition – this activity is part of the industry you operate in, that activity is not – can in itself place strategy development in a straitjacket. Pioneering companies succeed by redefining industry boundaries.

But this critique can be addressed by further segmentation – you can return to Chapter 1 and redefine your key product/market segments to allow for shifting boundaries.

Other critics have promoted the corporate environment (government, the regulatory framework, pressure groups, etc.) as a sixth force. Fine, stick in an extra box and arrow in the diagram if that helps you analyse your industry. Use Porter's five forces as a starting point in your strategy development, not the end point.

Assigning customer purchasing criteria

'All business success rests on something labeled a sale, which at least momentarily weds company and customer', wrote Tom Peters.

But why does that customer buy from that company? That is the question.

What do customers in one of your business's main segments need from you and your competitors? Are they looking for the lowest possible price for a given level of product or service? The highest quality product or service irrespective of price? Something in between?

Do customers have the same needs in your other business segments? Do some customer groups place greater importance on certain needs?

What exactly do they want in terms of product or service? The highest specifications? The fastest delivery? The most reliable? The best technical back-up? The most sympathetic customer service?

Customer needs from their suppliers are called customer purchasing criteria (CPCs). For business-to-business (or B2B) companies, CPCs typically include product quality (including features, performance and reliability), product range, delivery capabilities, technical support, customer service, relationship, reputation, financial stability, and so forth. And, of course, price.

For business-to-consumer (or B2C) companies, CPCs tend to be similar, though typically with less emphasis on product range and financial stability. Depending on the product or service being offered, the consumer will place varying importance on quality, service and price.

CPCs can usefully be grouped into six categories. They are customer needs relating to the:

▓ *Effectiveness* of the product (or service)
▓ *Efficiency* of the product
▓ *Range* of products provided
▓ *Relationship* with the producer
▓ *Premises* (only applicable if the customer needs to visit the supplier's premises)
▓ *Price*.

They can be conveniently remembered, with perhaps a faint redolence of a cult science fiction film, as the *E2-R2-P2* of customer purchasing criteria (see Table 4.1 in the essential case study).

Let's look briefly at each in turn.

E1: Effectiveness

The first need of any customer from any product or service is that the job gets done. You, the customer, have specific requirements on the features, performance and reliability of the product. You want the job done. Not half-done, not over-done, just done.

Whether you are the customer of a B2B or B2C supplier, you demand an effective solution. Depending on the nature of the product or service, your criteria may well include:

▓ Quality
▓ Design

- Features
- Specifications
- Functionality
- Reliability.

Some of these criteria will overlap. You should select two to four effectiveness criteria which are most pertinent to customer needs in your industry.

E2: Efficiency

The second main customer purchasing criteria heading is efficiency. The customer wants to receive the product or get the job done on time.

All customers place *some* level of importance on efficiency for all types of service. Different customer groups may place different levels of importance on efficiency for the same service.

In most B2B industries, efficiency here translates to delivery – or to customer service at the point of pick-up at the depot. In most B2C industries, efficiency equates to getting the product to the customer or delivering the service to schedule.

R1: Range

The range of products or services provided is an area customers can find important for some products or services, even most important, and for others of no importance at all.

R2: Relationship

Your supplier does the job and does it quickly. But do you like them? Is that important? The relationship component in providing a service should never be underestimated.

P1: Premises

This only applies to those businesses, typically services, where the buying decision can be influenced by the environment of the sale. Do you need a storefront for your business? What do customers expect of your premises?

P2: Price

Price is always an important CPC. Set your prices sky high and you won't have many customers. Set them too low and you won't stay in business.

Think about the buying decisions you make regularly and the influence of price. For non-essential goods or services, we tend to be price sensitive. For essential services, we tend to be less fixated with price. When your central heating system breaks down in the middle of winter, will you go for the cheapest service engineer? Or will you call around to find someone who is reliable, arrives when he says he will, fixes it with no fuss, and charges a price that is not necessarily cheap but at least is no rip-off?

You need to find out which of the above E2-R2-P2 of CPCs are important to your customers, in each key product/market segment. How important is each one, relative to others? How does their perception of importance vary by segment? Why?

You must also find out how your customers' needs are likely to change in the future. If they believe one purchasing criterion is highly important now, will it be as important in a few years' time? You need to know.

Finding out CPCs

All this is very well in theory, you may ask, but how do you know what customers want? Simple. Ask them!

It doesn't take long. You'd be surprised how after just a few discussions with any one customer group a predictable pattern begins to emerge. Some may consider one need 'very important', others just 'important'. But it's unlikely that another will say that it's 'unimportant'. Customers tend to have the same needs.

The comprehensive way to find out customer needs is through 'structured interviewing', where you ask a selected sample of customers a carefully prepared list of questions.

In developing a strategy for your business, a structured customer survey is an essential input. If you haven't done one recently, you would be well advised to conduct one. The Appendix shows how this is done.

Essential tip

Some customers may have a hidden agenda. They see a customer survey meeting as an opportunity to get you to nudge down your prices. Or to improve your service offering, incurring extra cost, without increasing pricing. They may say they rate price as the most important CPC even though they are primarily concerned with product quality.

Bear this in mind. It is business, and human nature. Such hidden agendas do not negate the validity of the customer survey. But judgement is required.

Deriving key success factors

What do firms in your industry need to do to succeed? What factors are key to success?

These are Key Success Factors (KSFs). They are what firms need to get right to satisfy customer purchasing criteria (CPCs) *and* run a sound business.

Typical KSFs are product (or service) quality, consistency, availability, range and product development (R&D). On the service side, KSFs can include distribution capability, sales and marketing effectiveness, customer service and post-sale technical support.

Other KSFs relate to the cost side of things, such as location of premises, scale of operations, state-of-the-art, cost-effective equipment and operational process efficiency.

To identify which are the most important KSFs for each of your main business segments, you need to undertake these steps:

- Convert CPCs into KSFs
  - Differentiation-related
  - Cost-related
- Assess two more KSFs
  - Management
  - Market share
- Apply weights to the KSFs
- Identify any must-have KSFs.

Let's look briefly at each of these steps.

Convert CPCs into KSFs

Here we convert the CPCs we researched above into KSFs. In other words, we work out *what your business has to do to meet those CPCs*.

KSFs are often the flipside to CPCs. Functionality may be a CPC, so R&D is a KSF. Reliability may be a CPC, so quality control is a KSF. Delivery to schedule may be a CPC, so spare capacity and/or manufacturing efficiency are KSFs. These are differentiation-related KSFs.

There's one CPC that needs special attention, and that's price. Customers of most services expect a keen *price*. Producers need to keep their *costs* down. Price is a CPC; cost competitiveness is a KSF.

Determinants of cost competitiveness in your business could include location of facilities, cost of materials, operational efficiency, use of subcontractors, outsourcing of business processes, overhead control, remuneration levels and IT systems.

And size may be important. Other things being equal, the larger the business, the lower costs should be *for each unit* of business sold. These are 'economies of scale' (see text box) and may apply not just to the unit cost of materials or other variable costs, where a larger business will benefit from negotiated volume discounts, but also to overheads, such as marketing, where the same expense on, for example, a magazine advertisement or trade show participation can be spread over a larger revenue base.

Assess two more KSFs

We have derived two sets of KSFs from the CPCs set out in the previous tool: differentiation-related and cost-related. There are two more sets to be considered: management and market share.

How important is management in general in your industry? Think about whether a well-managed company, with a superb sales and marketing team reinforced by an efficient operations team, but with an average product, would outperform a poorly managed company with a superb product in your industry.

There's one final KSF – an important one – that we need to take into account that isn't directly derived from a CPC: market share. The larger the market share, the stronger should be the provider.

A high market share can manifest itself in a number of different competitive advantages. One such area is in lower unit costs, but we've already covered this under economies of scale in cost-related KSFs, so we must be careful not to double-count.

Market share is an indicator of the breadth and depth of your customer relationships and your business reputation. Since it is more difficult to gain a new customer than to do repeat business with an existing customer, the provider with the larger market share typically has a competitive advantage – *the power of the incumbent.*

The power of the incumbent rises in proportion to the switching costs – not just the financial costs, but the time, hassle and even emotional costs. It's less of a wrench to change your printer than your accountant.

Apply weights to the KSFs

You've worked out which are the most important KSFs in your business. Each one has been ranked in order of importance. Now you need to weight them.

A simple quantitative approach works best. Don't worry, you won't have to compute a weighting of, say, 14.526%. That would be spurious accuracy. But it's helpful to derive a percentage for the weighting, whether to the nearest 5 or even 10%, so that in the next building block you can easily tot up and rate your firm's *overall* competitiveness.

So that 14.526% would become simply 15%. No more accuracy than that is needed. How to do it? There are two ways: methodically or by eyeballing.

If you want a systematic approach, take a look at one such in the text box. If you would prefer to eyeball it, to get a rough and ready answer, start from this guideline: market share 20%, cost factors 30%, management and differentiation factors 50%. Then adjust them to what you have found to be critical to success in your business. And make sure that however you jiggle them they still add up to 100%.

A systematic approach for deriving KSF weightings

Here's a step-by-step systematic approach to weighting KSFs:

1   Use judgement on the power of the incumbent to derive a weighting for market share of *i*%, typically in the range of 15 to 25%.

2   Revisit the importance of price to the customer. If you judged the customer need to be of medium importance, give cost

competitiveness a weighting of 20–25%. If low, give it 15–20%; if high, 35+%. If yours is a commodity business, it could be 40–45%, with a correspondingly low weighting for relative market share. Settle on c%.

3   Think on the importance of management factors to the success of your business, especially marketing. Settle on m%, typically within a 0–10% range.

4   You've now used up a total of $(i + c + m)$% of your available weighting.

5   The balance, namely $100 - (i + c + m) = D$%, will be the total weighting for differentiation factors.

6   Revisit the list of KSFs relating to differentiation issues, excluding price, which has already been covered under cost factors. Where you've judged a factor to be of low importance, give it a KSF score of 1; where high, 5. Rate pro rata for in between (for example, medium/high would be a 4).

7   Add up the total score for these differentiation-related KSFs (excluding price) = T.

8   Assign weightings to each differentiation KSF as follows: weighting (%) = KSF score divided by T, multiplied by D.

9   Round each weighting up or down to the nearest 5%.

10   Adjust further if necessary so that the sum of all KSF weights is 100%.

11   Eyeball them for sense, make final adjustments.

12   Check that the sum is still 100%.

Once you've eyeballed the weightings in general, you need to assess whether these weightings differ for each of your business segments. In particular, different customer groups can often place a different emphasis on price, so cost competitiveness may be more of an issue in one segment than in others. Other customers in other business segments may be more concerned about product quality or customer service.

Identify any must-have KSFs

There is one final wrinkle. But it may be crucial.

Is one of the KSFs in your business so important that if you don't rank highly against it you shouldn't even be in business? You simply won't begin to compete, let alone succeed? You won't win any business, or you won't be able to deliver on the business you win? In other words, it's a *must-have* KSF, rather than a mere *should-have*.

Must a business in your marketplace have, for example, the right ISO classification to win future orders in a competitively intensifying environment? Must it deploy the new cost-revolutionary range of capital equipment? Must your product incorporate a particular new feature?

Are any of the KSFs in your industry must-haves? Bear this in mind when assessing your competitive position in Chapter 5.

Essential tip

Don't end up with too many KSFs or you may lose the wood for the trees. Market share, management, two or three cost-related factors and five or six differentiation-related factors should be fine – a total of 10 or so.

Essential tool

Economies of scale

Size matters.

Correction: size matters in certain sectors, less so in others.

Another correction: even in sectors where size matters, smaller players can survive – if they are nimble.

In general, a company producing 1000 widgets a day will typically have higher costs *per unit* than one producing 2000 a day, and way higher unit costs than the market leader, which churns out 20,000 a day.

These are economies of scale, of which there are four main types, spread across the value chain (see Chapter 5):

■ *Purchasing economies*. The larger the producer, the more likely they will be able to drive a harder bargain with suppliers, such as steel producers, and enjoy volume discounts.

■ *Technical economies*. The machinery needed to produce

20,000 widgets a day is unlikely to be 20 times as expensive as that needed to produce 1000 a day.

▓ *Efficiency economies*. The process for producing 20,000 widgets a day is likely to be more highly automated, from handling inputs through manufacturing to handling outputs, and with more advanced or streamlined business processes, for example in R&D, than for the smaller plant.

▓ *Indivisibility economies*. Some items are beyond the reach of the smaller producer to buy, whether state-of-the-art equipment or a nationwide television advertisement.

Economies of scale apply as much to service businesses as in manufacturing, and to small as much as to global businesses.

Think of two hair salons competing on your local high street. One has double the amount of space as the other and serves on average 80 customers a day, compared to its smaller neighbour's 40. They are thus equally productive. They charge similar prices, yet the larger salon has lower rental costs per customer due to a deal negotiated with the landlord when the business doubled the amount of space leased. The larger salon also pays lower marketing costs per customer, since advertising space in the Yellow Pages or in the local glossy magazine costs the same per column inch for both salons, irrespective of how many customers the advertiser serves.

Magnify those businesses a million fold and advertising spending by, say, Guinness *per pint sold* will tend to be well below that of a niche brewer such as Cobra.

Nevertheless Cobra survives by offering a differentiated, premium-priced product – see the generic strategies of Chapter 7.

How important are economies of scale in your sector? Are there purchasing, technical, efficiency or indivisibility economies?

Have you placed sufficient credence on economies of scale when applying weights to the cost-related key success factors in your industry? Should you revisit that weighting?

Will you be able to exploit future economies of scale in your business as it grows?

Essential example

Jessops is shuttered

The decimation of the global main street continues apace. In the UK, the travails of the likes of Blockbuster, Comet, HMV and Jessops at the turn of 2013, to add those earlier in the post-crash recession of Adams, Barratts, Borders, Clinton, Game, Habitat, JJB, Oddbins and others, high streets may be en route to becoming mere service centres, featuring estate agents, financiers, hair stylists and caterers. The last physical goods left may soon be at vanity boutiques, convenience stores or discount/charity shops.

The demise of camera specialist Jessops seemed especially sad. The writing was always on the wall for the music and film merchants – online downloading, whether legal or illegal in the days before iTunes, was the classic substitute force among Porter's five. When fierce competition from online retailers and supermarkets was added to the mix, the likes of Our Price, Tower, Woolworth's, Zavvi and, more recently, HMV were truly up against it.

But cameras cannot be downloaded. And they are a more complex sale than compact discs, requiring patient explanation by the sales assistant of the merits of different types of lens, speed, memory, battery life and so forth of one unit versus the next. Surely there remained a rationale for a Jessops on the UK high street?

Perhaps not. Porter's five forces are aligned very much against the high street camera retailing industry:

- *Industry rivalry* – modest from direct competitors such as the department stores, though the economic doldrums are no help, but intense from online retailers like Amazon.

- *Barriers to entry* – theoretically low, other than in staff training, but practically very high, since few would choose to enter an industry in trouble.

- *Substitutes* – the killer, as for music retailing. Sure, cameras cannot be downloaded, but photos can, and mobile phones or tablets offering camera capability are now the norm. Lens quality has improved greatly, with 6, 8 or 12 megapixel camera phones sold routinely, and with Nokia even launching one of 41 megapixels; these phones have kiboshed the market for simple point-and-shoot digital cameras, forcing high street camera retailers to focus on higher quality, more expensive, slower-moving units.

■ *Customer power* – another killer, with too many customers treating the Jessops staff as technical advisers, then walking out of the shop to check online prices on their smartphones.

■ *Supplier power* – it was very much in the interests of Jessops' two main suppliers, Canon and Nikon, for the firm to thrive, and they gave much support during its early difficulties; ultimately, however, trading performance forced them to tighten their credit terms, leaving the company with little option other than administration.

There are times when all of Porter's five forces seem to be conspiring against the industry players – and that has been very true for many retail subsectors since the 2008 financial crash, including cameras. Not all is gloom, though – the forces have been aligned right behind one retail subsector, the pound shop!

Gauging competition in a start-up

Too many start-up business plans are based on the premise that theirs is a new concept. Competition is non-existent, or irrelevant.

In the vast majority of cases, this presumption is both wrong and dangerous. At best it is only ever partially true.

There is always some competition. Whatever is your solution to the perceived needs of the customer, someone else, somewhere else, has another solution.

Or they will have. If they don't have a solution now, they may well do so once they have seen yours.

So we'll look at three aspects of competition in a start-up:

■ Direct competition
■ Indirect competition
■ Competitive response.

Direct competition

If your new venture is a business with a clearly defined existing marketplace, then your Chapter 4 analysis will be no different from that of an established business.

You'll identify the competitors, soon to be augmented by one, and assess competitive intensity, soon to be intensified perhaps by your firm's entry.

An example, as previously introduced in Chapter 3, would be a start-up boutique specialising in designer childrenswear on the High Street. Your competitors would include other such boutiques, any boutiques focusing on adult clothes but also offering a selection for children, childrenswear chainstores, the childrenswear departments of department stores, and all of these variants using different routes to market, for example catalogue shopping or the Internet.

You will be entering a highly competitive market – retail can be an unforgivingly competitive arena – but hopefully with a distinctive edge that you will set out forcefully in Chapter 5.

Indirect competition

What if your idea is a new concept? Who are your competitors?

They are whoever was providing an alternative solution to the customer before your business existed, competing for a similar share of the customer's wallet as you are.

Suppose you invented an ingenious wooden roller-ball back-massaging device which released aromatherapeutic oils as you massaged. It's new, it's unique, it's brilliant, it works!

But it has competition. The customer's need is relief from back tension or pain. The customer is prepared to dip into her pocket to relieve that pain.

She has a range of alternative solutions – other wooden roller-ball devices, plastic and metal versions, electrically powered massage devices, massage chairs. She can go to a masseur, even an aromatherapist. She can purchase the oils and self-administer. She can take pills.

All these are competitors, even if only indirect ones. Yours will occupy a particular price positioning – above basic roller-ball devices, below power-driven ones – but the customer has the option to trade up or down.

In the next chapter, you'll consider the pros of alternative solutions from their perspective and the cons from yours. You'll lay out your stall. But it's a stall in relation to the alternative providers – and these competitors need to be identified in this chapter and the intensity of this competition needs to be assessed.

Competitive response

What will be the reaction of competitors, direct and indirect, if your venture turns out to be a success? You cannot assume that they will stand idly by and cheer you on.

If your new concept is patent protected, that is great. Your backer will need to know full details.

But there are ways for a competitor to negotiate a path around a patent, and legally. Offering a slight variant on the theme can often be enough.

How will you respond, not if but when your competitors respond to your market entry?

Suppose your childrenswear boutique is successful. How will the department store down the road respond? Perhaps by cordoning off the childrenswear department, refitting the design, engaging a clown every Saturday morning? How would you respond to that response?

Suppose your oil-infused roller-ball massaging device was successful? How will producers of basic devices respond? Will they copy the device if unpatented? If patented, could they offer their devices along with free-standing oils for self-administering at 15% below your price? How would you respond to that?

Consider competitive response. And prepare your return response.

Essential tip

If your firm fares well, it will ring a bell – for the competitor as for the customer.

Industry competition risks and opportunities

You have assessed competitive intensity in your industry, both now and over the next few years. What are the risks to that assessment? What could happen to intensify competition further?

What could happen to internal rivalry, to customer bargaining power or to any of the other forces to intensify competition?

What is the likelihood of those risks occurring? And what would be the impact if they did?

As defined in Chapter 3, what are the 'big' risks, those which are reasonably likely and with reasonable impact?

How will you mitigate these big risks should they occur?

Conversely, what are the big opportunities to hopefully surpass these risks? And how will you exploit them should they occur?

Essential case study

Extramural Ltd Strategic Review, 2013

Chapter 4: Industry competition

Richard and Jane Davies are only too aware that their arch rival, ActivTours, is the market leader in the school activity tour business. First to enter the market, with a top-quality offering, now with 15 centres and 34% market share and with the respect the name conveys commanding a price premium, ActivTours has been the one to beat for all subsequent entrants. Yet Extramural (with 23% share), Student Tours Ltd (STL, on 14%) and a range of others have each found ways of carving out slices of the market, with varying degrees of profitability.

In educational tours, STL is the market leader by some distance with 45%, followed by EduTours (owned by ActivTours) on 21% and a range of smaller players, including Extramural on 8%. The day camp market, however, has a different line-up, with neither ActivTours nor STL present and three specialist players, Ultra Camps, KoolKamps and Monkeys, sharing two-thirds of the market. Extramural, a recent entrant, has taken 5% to date.

The Davieses apply rigorously Porter's five forces model and derive these conclusions on the school activity tours market (see Figure 4.2):

■ With the industry maturing, demand contracting in 2009–10 and significant barriers to entry, such as customer confidence, proven safety provision, teacher loyalty and, increasingly, the limited availability of suitable sites, the threat of new entrants remains modest – unlike in the 2000s, when the fast-growing market attracted a number of players undeterred by the barriers and eager to jump them.

■ Ease of substitution remains high – should anything go amiss in the industry, teachers could readily redirect their Year 6 children to other, arguably safer activity trips, such as camping, hiking or team sports, or to less active alternatives such as educational tours.

■ Internal rivalry, unprecedently high during the 2009–12 demand contraction, should ease with a return to economic growth, especially during the fiercely contested off-peak and shoulder months – though competition for the best leased sites for peak season demand may well get tougher as demand recovers.

■ Suppliers may take advantage of increased demand for the best leased sites and push prices back up to 2008 levels and beyond.

■ Customers are as loyal as can be found in any industry, given the administrative burden teachers have to bear to shift supplier, but school budgets have been under severe pressure and governors may insist on schools getting value for money.

Overall, the Davieses find the school activity tours industry to be of medium competitive intensity, tougher than it used to be in the halcyon days of the 1990s and 2000s – though they would take a medium over a high any day. Competition seems set to intensify modestly over the next few years due to a probable increase in bargaining power of both suppliers and customers. There may therefore be an element of downward pressure on industry pricing – something Richard and Jane will have to factor into their budget and business plan.

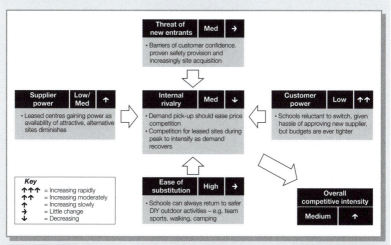

Figure 4.2   **Extramural Ltd: industry competition in school activity tours**

Next they turn their attention to customer purchasing criteria (CPCs). They meet their customers regularly and feel that they know what their customers need, and have needed over the years – but nevertheless read with interest the results of their intern, Sasha's, customer survey of primary school teachers. Her main findings (see Table 4.1) are as follows.

■ Safety and security of the children remain paramount, above all other considerations – a *sine qua non* of doing business.

■ The quality of both facilities and instructors is very important.

■ Teaching capabilities are important for combined learning/ activity tours, whether in ICT, environmental science or languages – though obviously of no relevance if the customer seeks a purely activity-based tour.

■ Customer service and an enthusiastic attitude of all customer-facing staff are increasingly important, and a number of customers cited this as a major factor in deciding to rebook – a finding that Jane Davies highlights in yellow when reading it.

Table 4.1   **Extramural Ltd: customer purchasing criteria for school activity tours**

	Customer purchasing criteria	Importance	Change
Effectiveness	• Safety and security	***Highest***	→
	• Quality of activity facilities	*High*	→
	• Quality and training of instructors	*High*	→
	• Capabilities of teachers	*High or n/a*	→
	• Educational content	*High or n/a*	→
	• ICT content	*Low/Med*	→
Efficiency	• Planning and delivery to schedule	*Med*	→
Relationship	• Customer service through process	*Med/High*	↑
	• Enthusiasm	*Med/High*	↑
Range	• Range of activities	*High*	→
Premises	• Quality of housing and grounds	*Low*	→
Price	• Affordable to as many as possible	*Med/High*	↑

■ The quality of accommodation is less important than the range of facilities offered – this came as a bit of a surprise to the Davieses, having recently invested in upgrading accommodation in more than half of their centres.

■ Price was important, since teachers wanted the trip to be affordable to as many in their classes as possible, especially in these difficult economic times, but it was not the most important criterion.

The Davieses and Sasha then translate the CPCs into key success factors (KSFs), that is, what Extramural needs to do to meet customer needs and run a profitable business. They conclude (see Table 4.2):

Table 4.2   **Extramural Ltd: key success factors in school activity tours**

Customer purchasing criteria		Associated key success factors
Effectiveness	• Safety and security	• Safety and security
	• Quality of activity facitlites	
	• Quality of training of instructors	• Product quality
	• Capabilities of teacher	
	• Educational content in general	• Product innovation
	• ICT content	
Efficiency	• Planning and delivery to schedule	• Delivery
Relationship	• Customer service through process	• Customer service
		• Sales, marketing, CRM
	• Enthusiasm	• Staff training
Range	• Range of activities	• Product range
Premises	• Quality of housing and grounds	• Product quality
Price	• Affordability	• Cost competitiveness

- Safety and security represent a must-have KSF, a threshold which must be reached even to be in business.

- Safety and security provision above that threshold is a differentiating KSF, but one which is less important than some others.

- Product quality and range are the most important differentiating factors ...

- followed by customer service and delivery.

- Cost competitiveness, the KSF equivalent to the price CPC, is an important factor.

The Davieses ask Sasha to apply weights to the KSFs using the systematic approach recommended in this book. Here are her workings (see Table 4.3):

- In the school activity tour business, the incumbent has great power. Keep 60 children full of beans for one week and by the end of it the teacher in charge should have signed up for the same thing the following year – so a weighting of 20%.

- Cost competitiveness is of medium/high importance, so a weighting of 25% feels right, though it could arguably be 30%.

- Management factors, especially in sales, marketing and

Table 4.3 **Extramural Ltd: key success factor weighting in school activity tours**

Key Success Factors: School Activity Tours	Weighting
Market share	20%
Cost factors: Economies of scale, occupancy	25%
Management factors: Sales, marketing, CRM	10%
Differentiation factors: Safety and security	10%
Product quality and range	20%
Customer service and delivery	15%
Total	**100%**

customer relationship management, are important, so a weighting of 10%.

■ The weightings so far total 55%, leaving 45% to be shared among the differentiation factors.

■ Sasha apportions the differentiating factors by their relative importance as CPCs, giving:

– Safety and security 10%

– Product quality and range 20%

– Customer service and delivery 15%.

■ She checks the total – it is 100%.

The Davieses are now ready to rate Extramural's performance against these KSFs, including feeding in further results of Sasha's structured interview programme – but that is for the next chapter.

Essential checklist on gauging industry competition

Your strategy will have a much greater chance of success than at most other firms because you will devote a whole section to the analysis of competition. Remember the words of General Sun Tzu in the introduction to this book: strategy is to 'know your opponent'.

Why so many strategy presentations and business plans devote such little space to competition baffles me. The arrogance of the manager or entrepreneur in dismissing the relevance of competitive trends borders on the suicidal.

Instead you will analyse in depth your competitors and the intensity of competition. Detail the size, location, number of employees, product offering and so forth of your competitors. And assess how competitively intense your industry is, now and to come, by considering:

■ *The forces of internal rivalry* – including the size and number of players, demand growth, external pressures and barriers to exit

■ *The threat of new entrants* – describing barriers to entry

> ▨ *The threat of substitute products or services*
>
> ▨ *The bargaining power of customers* – often dependent on the relative numbers and scale of providers and customers
>
> ▨ *The bargaining power of suppliers* – likewise, but you are the customer.
>
> Assess in particular what is likely to happen to industry pricing given these forces of competitive intensity. Finally, highlight the main risks and opportunities around industry competition over the next few years.
>
> If yours is a business start-up with a new concept, identify competitors providing alternative solutions and analyse the industry accordingly. Consider how competitors may respond to your entry and how you in turn will retaliate.
>
> Against this backdrop, what will be customers' main purchasing criteria over the next few years?
>
> And what will your firm and your competitors need to do to meet those criteria and run a successful business – what will be the key success factors?

5

Tracking competitive advantage

" If you don't have a competitive advantage, don't compete.

Jack Welsh

In this chapter

- Rating competitive position
  - Essential tool: Product/market risk

- ▓ Reviewing resources and capabilities
  - Essential tool: The value chain
- ▓ Creating competitive advantage in a start-up

You have built the foundation of the strategy pyramid. The micro-economic context is set. Now you need to place your firm within that context.

You need to set out your firm's competitive position and pinpoint your competitive advantage – for each main business segment. And track it over time.

You also need to do the same for all your main competitors.

Then you need to assess the strategic importance of your firm's resources and capabilities.

These are your main challenges in this building block, the tracking of competitive advantage.

Rating competitive position

In the last chapter you determined what would be the key factors needed for success in your main business segments over the next few years.

How does your firm rate against those each of key success factors (KSFs)?

How do your principal competitors rate?

How is your overall competitive position in each main segment? And theirs? How do your relative positions differ by segment?

You need to rate your competitive position, and that of each principal competitor, over time and for each main segment.

You could do this right now, at your desk, based on feedback you and your sales and purchasing teams have received from customers and suppliers over the years. Or you could do it more methodically, via a structured interviewing programme (see the Appendix).

In this analysis you will assess your strengths and weaknesses and those of your peers. It will pinpoint your source of competitive advantage – as well as that of your most formidable competitors.

The process of rating competitive position is straightforward. Use a 0–5 rating system. If you perform about the same as your peers against a KSF, give yourself a score in the middle, a 3 (*good, favourable*). If you perform very strongly, even dominantly, a 5 (*very strong*). If poorly, a 1 (*weak*). If you perform not quite as well as most others, give yourself a 2 (*tenable*). If better than most, a 4 (*strong*).

Now do the same for each of your principal competitors against that KSF. Who's the best performer against this KSF? Do they merit a 5, or are they better but not *that* much better than others, for a 4? And so on, against each KSF.

If you've used Excel, your competitive position literally falls out at the bottom of the spreadsheet. Your overall rating is the sum of each rating (r) against each KSF multiplied by the percentage weighting (w) of the KSF. If there are n KSFs, your overall rating will be (r1 * w1) + (r2 * w2) + (r3 * w3) + ... + (rn + wn). As long as the percentage weightings add up to 100%, you should get the right answer.

Table 5.1 gives an example taken from a recent strategy assignment. It shows that the company was the leading player in its niche UK engineering market, but there was no room for complacency. The company had the largest presence in the market, the best engineering service network and a strong cost base, but competitor A had developed a product with enhanced features and functionality that was proving attractive to customers.

Table 5.1 Competitive position: an example

Key success factors in UK engineering niche market	Weighting	The company	Competitor A	Competitor B
Market share	15%	5	3.3	2
Cost factors	35%	4	3.5	2.5
Differentiation factors: Product capability and range	15%	4	4.5	3
Product reliability	15%	4	4	2.5
Engineering service network	10%	5	3.5	2.5
Customer service	10%	3	3	2
Competitive position	**100%**	**4.2**	**3.6**	**2.5**

Key: 1 = Weak, 2 = Tenable, 3 = Favourable, 4 = Strong, 5 = Dominant

Competing by segment

Apply the same process for each key product/market segment: identify how customer purchasing criteria differ by segment, assess key success factors for each, and derive the competitive position in each. You'll find that some positions will vary due to weighting. Take product quality: your rating against that KSF may well be the same in each segment relating to a product group. But its weighting may differ by customer group segment, thereby impacting your overall competitive position in each.

Ratings for the same KSF may well differ by segment. For instance, your company may have an enviable track record in service and repair in one segment, but you haven't long been in another – rating a 5 in the first but only a 2 in the other. Again that will filter down to the bottom line of competitive position.

Competing over time

So far your analysis of competitive position has been static. You've rated your firm's current competitiveness and those of others. But that's only the first part of the story. How has your competitive position changed over the last few years and how is it likely to change over the next few years? You need to understand the dynamics. Is it set to improve or worsen?

The simplest way to do this is to add an extra column to your chart, representing your position in, say, three years' time. Then you can build in any improvements in your ratings against each KSF. These prospective improvements need, for the time being, to be both in the pipeline and likely. In the next chapter we shall assess how you can proactively and systematically improve your competitive position. That's strategy. But for now it is useful to see how your competitive position seems set to evolve naturally over the next few years, assuming no significant change in strategy.

Remember, however, that improved competitive position is a two-edged sword. Your competitors too will have plans. This is where analysis of KSF dynamics gets challenging. It's easy enough to know what you're planning, but what are your competitors up to?

Try adding a couple of further columns representing your two most fearsome competitors as they may be in three years' time. Do you have any idea what they're planning to do to improve their competitiveness in the near future? What are they likely to do? What could they do? *What are you afraid they'll do?*

Table 5.2   Future competitive position: an example

Key success factors in UK engineering niche market	Weighting	The company today	Competitor A today	Competitor A tomorrow
Relative market share	15%	5	3.3	4
Cost factors	35%	4	3.5	4
Differentiation factors: Product capability and range	15%	4	4.5	4.5
Product reliability	15%	4	4	4
Engineering service network	10%	5	3.5	4
Customer service	10%	3	3	3.5
Competitive position	100%	4.2	3.6	4.0

Key: 1 = Weak, 2 = Tenable, 3 = Favourable, 4 = Strong, 5 = Dominant

Returning to the example of the UK niche engineering company, management was aware that competitor A had plans to outsource certain components and reduce cost and set up a joint venture to enhance its engineering service capability. A's strategy seemed set to narrow the competitive gap unless my client deployed a proactive strategy focusing on R&D – see Table 5.2.

Getting past first base

In the last chapter, we introduced the concept of the must-have KSF, in which without a good rating your business cannot even begin to compete.

Did you find a must-have KSF in any of your business segments? If so, how do you rate against it? Favourable, strong? Fine. Okay-ish? Questionable. Weak? Troublesome. A straight zero, not even a 1? You're out. You don't get past first base.

And what about in a few years' time? Could any KSF develop into a must-have? How will you rate then? Will you get past first base?

And even though you rate as tenable against a must-have KSF today, might it slip over time? Could it slide below 2, into tricky territory?

This may be a case of being cruel to be kind. It's better to know. The sooner you realise that you're in a wrong business segment, the sooner you can withdraw and focus resources on the right segments.

Implications for future market share

This competitive position analysis plays a useful role in business planning. It gives you an idea of how your firm is likely to fare over the next few years *in relation to the market as a whole.*

If your overall competitive position turns out to be around 3, or good/favourable, you should, other things being equal, be able to grow business *in line with the market* over the next few years. In other words, to hold market share.

If it is around 4 or above, you should be able to *beat the market,* to gain market share, again, other things being equal. Suppose you forecast market demand growth of 10% a year in Tool 17. With a competitive position of 4, you should feel comfortable that you can grow your business at, say, 12–15% a year.

If your competitive position is around 2, however, you'll be less confident about your business prospects. It's more likely you'll *underperform the market* and, if your boss is expecting the firm to outpace the market, something will have to change!

Implications for strategy development

Competitive position analysis also throws up some facts and judgements highly useful for strategy development:

- How you compete overall in key segments – hence where you are most likely to be most profitable relative to the competition
- Areas of strength in key segments, which can be built on
- Areas of weakness in some segments, which may need to be worked on
- Areas of strength or weakness common to many or all segments, which can be built or worked on
- Relative competitiveness in each key segment
- Change in competitiveness over time
- In summary, your source of competitive advantage, tracked over time.

It will form the basis for identification of the strategic gap in the next chapter.

Essential tip

Having used this competitive position tool for three decades and managed many junior consultants in its use, I offer three tips:

■ Too much analysis hinders decision-making – don't do this for too many segments, too many KSFs, too many competitors within each segment or too many years past and future. Keep it simple – opt for the main segments, the main KSFs, the main competitors, now and three years hence; look for the main findings, the key lessons; drill down further only if necessary and potentially illuminating.

■ Don't get too scientific – stick to the nearest whole number in the 0–5 range, or when you are torn between a 3 and a 4 then go for 3.5. The exception is for market share, which lends itself to more precise quantification – if your firm has 55% share, competitor A has 25% and B has 20%, give yourself a 5 but don't give A a 3 and B a 2, be more precise: give A a proportionate 2.3 and B a 1.8.

■ Always have a first shot with or without the relevant research, but if you feel uncomfortable about a rating, type it provisionally into Excel in red or in italics and undertake to do the required research, benchmarking with competitors, for example, or conducting a customer survey, before firming up the rating.

Circumnavigate these pitfalls and the analysis is invaluable.

Essential tool

Product/market risk

Igor Ansoff, author of the first book exclusively on corporate strategy, published in 1965, created his product/market matrix to illustrate the inherent risks of four generic growth strategies – growth through market penetration, market development, product development and diversification.

He argued that diversification, straying too far from what you best know, is by far the riskiest strategy.

Here is how to apply it. Draw a 2 × 2 matrix, with existing and new products along the *x*-axis and existing and new markets along the *y*-axis – see Figure 5.1. Take your main sales initiatives planned for the next three to five years and place them in the relevant quadrant, along with their proportionate contribution to the overall forecast sales increase in that period.

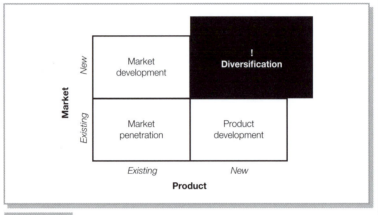

Figure 5.1   **The product/market matrix**

Source: Adapted from Ansoff, Igor H., 'Strategies for Diversification',
Harvard Business Review, Sept–Oct 1957

Which quadrant shows the greatest forecast uplift in sales? If it is in existing products to existing or new markets, or in new products to existing markets, there should be no due cause for alarm. If it is the quadrant of new products to new markets, that is another story.

A diversification strategy, that of growth through launching new products into new markets, operates on a higher plane of risk from the other three strategies. Superficially attractive, it is highly risky. While the first three strategies build on familiar skills in production, purchasing, sales and marketing, this is unlikely to be the case with diversification. Furthermore, diversification stands the risk of absorbing a disproportionately high proportion of managerial and operational resources, due simply to the lack of familiarity with the new venture.

In later years, Ansoff came to believe that the matrix was an oversimplification, due to the different degrees of risk associated with new *market segment* entry and new *country market* entry. So he introduced a third dimension to allow for new geography. Thus his two-dimensional 2 × 2 matrix became 3D, a 2 × 2 × 2 cuboid.

The extremes of risk are now highlighted even more. The greater the diversification, the greater the compounded risk. The risk of pursuing a strategy of a new product serving a new market segment in a new geographic market is of a very different order of magnitude from a strategy of further market penetration by an existing product in an existing market segment in an existing geographical market.

This simple matrix helps to crystallise the riskiness of a proposed strategy. You should always be conscious of the *compounding* effect on risk from a growth strategy premised on new products *and* new markets *and* new geographies.

Reviewing resources and capabilities

How strategically important is whatever your firm does well?

You need to put your firm's resources and capabilities into perspective. Rate them by two criteria – how important they are relative to each other and how strongly you are placed relative to the competition.

You should start by differentiating between your firm's resources and capabilities. Resources are the productive assets owned by the firm, whether tangible, intangible or human. Capabilities are what the firm does with its resources, how it deploys them.

Land, buildings, plant and equipment are resources. So too are intangible resources such as brand and personnel. How they work together organisationally and operationally, whether in production, purchasing, product development, sales or marketing, are the firm's capabilities.

Use a three-step approach on appraising resources and capabilities and thereby guiding strategy development:

1 Identify key resources and capabilities.
2 Appraise them
   – Assess their relative importance
   – Assess your relative strengths
   – Bring the appraisal together.
3 Develop strategy implications.

In the first step, translate the key success factors you established in Chapter 4 into specific resources and capabilities. For this, you may find value chain analysis of help – see the text box.

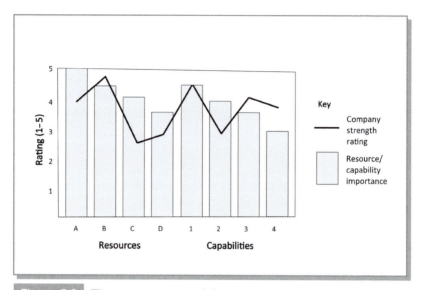

Figure 5.2   **The resource strength/importance matrix**

Source: Adapted from Robert M. Grant, *Contemporary Strategy Analysis,* Blackwell, 7th edition, 2011

Then you rate them by degree of importance, as defined by which resources or capabilities are the more important in conferring competitive advantage. Try rating them on a scale of 1–5.

Next you assess how your firm stacks up against the competition in each of these resources and capabilities. Again, you can use a scale of 1–5.

Now you can translate these ratings onto a comb chart – see Figure 5.2. Resources (represented by columns) are set out in descending order of importance, followed by the same for capabilities.

Next you insert your firm's strength rating against each resource and capability. Join up the points and you have a toothcomb shape.

Hopefully, your firm will be strong in areas of strategic importance, suggesting competitive advantage. If not, that suggests strategic weakness. If you are strong in an area of lesser importance, like capability – number 4 in the chart – that may be a superfluous strength.

Finally, you can develop the strategic implications of the process. How can you exploit the key strengths displayed – perhaps by further targeted investment in developing capabilities? How can you manage the key weaknesses – perhaps through outsourcing? To what extent can the superfluous strengths be deployed to greater effect on shareholder value – perhaps through divestment?

Essential tip

Take care. Successful companies are not necessarily those that possess the greater resources, but those that make best use of the resources they have. And working on weaknesses may not give as good a return as building on strengths – see Chapter 7.

Essential tool

The value chain

Are there weak links in your business?

Michael Porter's value chain is a tool for identifying key processes in your business, assessing your firm's competitive capabilities in each and thereby assessing wherein lies the source of your competitive advantage.

Porter divides a firm's activities into primary and support activities – see Figure 5.3. Primary activities involve the conversion of a range of inputs to the production process through to the delivery of the output to the customer and beyond. Or, in the case of a service business, they involve the conversion of personnel and

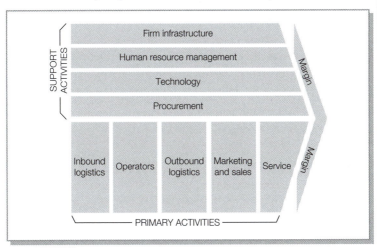

Figure 5.3   **The value chain**

Source: Adapted from Porter, M.E., *Competitve Advantage* (The Free Press, 2004)

their work tools through the operational processes to service delivery and after-sales service.

Primary activities are:

- *Inbound logistics* – those required to receive, store and disseminate inputs
- *Operations* – those required to transform inputs into outputs
- *Outbound logistics* – those required to collect, store and distribute the output
- *Marketing and sales* – those required to generate awareness of the firm's outputs and their benefits and to stimulate customers to buy them
- *Service* – those required to maintain effective working of the product or service post-sale.

Support activities are those which apply across the range of primary activities. They are:

- *The firm's infrastructure* – those required to serve the firm's general needs, typically centred around HQ, such as accounting, finance, legal, planning, PR and general management
- *Human resource management* – those required to recruit, hire, train, develop, compensate and (as necessary) discipline or dismiss personnel
- *Technology* – those required to research and develop the equipment, hardware, software and processes needed in all primary activities
- *Procurement* – those required to acquire inputs needed in all primary activities.

How does your firm rate in each link? How do your principal competitors rate?

What insights does value chain analysis throw up for your competitive position analysis?

Essential example

The everlasting Monsoon

I too go shopping. I accompany my wife into the lashing winds and biting cold of the streets of Kingston-upon-Thames in the après-Christmas sale, trekking from one ladies' fashion store to another looking for bargains in coats and jackets. I soak up the buzz of this mass of humanity scrabbling for goodies, quaintly reminiscent of the Arab souk or the Thai night market. But by the 61st minute the environment starts to oppress. I start to crave the family hearth, the mug of tea, the mince pie. That's shopping done for the year.

But there is one store it is always a pleasure to dip into. How Monsoon is still standing there on the High Street defies the imagination. It is a throwback to my youth. Its racks teem with brightly coloured, highly decorative, often bejewelled garments of unmistakeably Asian influence. Unmistakeably posh hippy. Unmistakeably 60s/70s.

Peter Simon was like many of us young adults at the time – rebellious, anti-authoritarian, anti-materialist, anti-fashion, pro-freedom, pro-love – think Beatles and Sergeant Pepper. He escaped to live in a commune by a nudist beach in the Balearic Islands and on his return set up a stall on London's Portobello Road selling sheepskin 'Afghan' jackets, which were pretty much *de rigueur* in bohemian circles at the time. Mine may even have been from his stall.

He took a few months off to head East overland on a VW bus on the then standard hippie trail from London to India, via Turkey, Iran and Afghanistan – a journey unthinkable, of course, since the Russian invasion of 1979. But whereas most travellers were content merely to admire and absorb the wondrous culture, history and philosophy of the region, Simon spotted a business opportunity.

He was struck by the colours of the dresses worn by the Rajasthani women, as well as the hand-crafted nature of the cotton, the cut, the block printing, the embroidery and the embellishment. He opened a store in Beauchamp Place, Knightsbridge, in 1973, selling a collection of clothes mainly sourced from India but tailored to the Western taste.

He had found a niche: clothes with an element of the exotic for the middle-class Western, liberal, would-be bohemian woman. And he stuck to it. Forty years on and Monsoon's competitive advantage is little different. In the company's own words:

> Monsoon is a brand with a highly distinctive identity. The intrinsic beauty of fabric, colour and technique so evident in the early sourcing of Monsoon's products from India, Afghanistan and the Far East, continues to exercise a strong influence. Today, Monsoon's team of talented designers gather inspiration and ideas from around the world to create the Monsoon signature look.

In the meantime he expanded, rolling out shops across the UK and overseas. He also found that his shops were selling exotic-looking accessories as fast as they were being stocked, so he opened up a specialist accessories boutique in the Piazza at Covent Garden. There are now more Accessorize than Monsoon stores.

From running a market stall in Portobello Road to chairing a privately owned, global chain with 400+ stores in the UK and 600+ more in 60+ other countries and sales of around £650m, while running homes in Chelsea, Paris, New York, Ibiza and Klosters, Peter Simon is an ex-hippy unlike the rest of us. He found his boho-chic niche and monetised it – in the lingo of the hippy era whence he emerged, funky freak turned badass breadhead?

Creating competitive advantage in a start-up

The process set out in this chapter is not that different for a start-up, whether serving an existing market or creating a new one. You need to assess your likely competitive position in the main segments where you intend to compete and develop a strategy to enhance that competitiveness over time.

There are three main differences:

- Your competitive position is in the future rather than the present tense.
- It will be affected adversely from the outset by a low rating against all key success factors pertaining to experience.

■ You must nevertheless have some evident competitive advantage just to survive in the early years.

Your competitive position in a new venture is a judgement more on the immediate future than on the present. For an established business, the debate revolves as much around the present and recent past as it does the future – around the weighting of KSFs and/or your ratings against specific KSFs, as justified by evidence from customer, supplier and other interviews, each of which will be based as much on fact and performance track record as on judgement.

But for a start-up, the debate will be partly conjecture, especially if your venture is to a new market. There is no track record of your performance, nor maybe on the market. For the latter, though, you must find evidence from any possible source – see Chapter 3.

There is nothing you can do about your new venture's rating against those KSFs which demand experience. Thus your rating against market share will be low at the outset, so too perhaps against some cost-related factors, especially that of scale.

Likewise your rating against some differentiation factors may be low. Your lack of track record may count against you in consistency of product quality, delivery, customer service, or sales and marketing.

In that case, how will your firm compete? The answer is that it's not easy being a new entrant in an existing market. Your competitive position will indeed be low relative to the leaders at the outset. But if you are addressing a growing market and/or you can differentiate your product or service sufficiently, things should improve. Your competitive position in three to five years' time should have improved measurably – your market share rating should be up, your unit costs down, your service performance improved.

But this analysis further highlights the importance of segmentation. If your new venture does not serve an existing market but creates its own, then all changes. The analysis of competition will be undertaken not for the market as a whole but for your addressed product/market segment. And if that is a new segment, created by your new venture, you effectively have no *direct* competition.

But there are two caveats:

■ You will have indirect competition, as discussed in Chapter 4, who may up their game if you are successful.

■ You will in due course face competition from new entrants, if your new market is worthy of pursuit.

To survive the hostile early years of a start-up, you must create a distinct competitive advantage. This can take a multitude of forms, including most commonly:

- A new product (or service)
- A similar product but at lower cost
- A similar product but with a distinct element of differentiation, whether in quality (features, functionality, reliability?), distribution (electronic rather than physical?), delivery, service (pre-sale help, after-sale care?) or marketing (a theme which resonates?)
- A similar product tailored to a new market
- A similar product offered to a new region.

Whatever your source of perceived competitive advantage, it must carry enough weight to give your new business at least a tenable competitive position in those early years of the venture.

If your venture manages no more than a rating of 1 out of 5 for market share (as is likely), 1.5 for cost factors (also likely in the early days), 2 for product quality, 2 for service and 2 for delivery, that will give you a start-up competitive position in the range of 1.5 to 1.8, depending on KSF weightings.

That is untenable. Your start-up has no distinct competitive advantage. It will fail.

If, however, you manage to earn a rating of 4 or even 5 against a couple of those KSFs, in those specific areas of your competitive advantage, your initial competitive position may emerge in the range 2.5 to 3.0 – which is not too bad for a start-up, given the inevitably low ratings against market share, cost factors and management in the early days. It is a tenable, bordering on a favourable, competitive position.

The key to a successful start-up, to repeat, is competitive advantage.

For further reading on competitive advantage in a start-up, try John Mullins' terrific book, *The New Business Road Test*. This is essential reading on all the preparatory work and research you should undertake before firming up a strategy for a start-up, especially in a new market.

Essential example

Of diet, dance and detectives

We saw above how Monsoon identified a competitive advantage and sustained it remarkably over four decades.

What real-life examples spring to your mind? Think of a company you admire. What is its competitive advantage? Is it sustainable?

I always enjoy on a Sunday evening turning to the back pages of the Sunday newspaper to read about some small company that has made it. By making it, I am not talking about an entrepreneur doing an Apple or a Facebook, but an entrepreneur surviving and earning enough for a comfortable lifestyle for the family.

The vast majority of businesses are small businesses. And it always saddens me to hear of one or the other going under. Each founder has shown such spirit, such initiative, such courage to set out on his or her own that few merit such a fate.

But often the failure of a small business comes about because it does not possess a sustainable competitive advantage. It is, in effect, a me-too business.

Here then, to end on a cheery note, are three lovely and lively examples of businesses whose founders created a memorable, sustainable competitive advantage:

▓ *Reggae Reggae sauce* – created by a Rasta reggae singer selling his spicy sauce by the side of the road at the Notting Hill Carnival. Its catchline of 'put some music in your food' has helped the sauce be sold nationwide and extended the brand into adjacent lines and prepared foods such as Reggae Reggae pizzas at Domino's.

▓ *Zumba* – created by a Colombian dance instructor who forgot his standard aerobics dance tapes one day, so he substituted his own tapes of salsa and merengue and found that his class loved it. He took his idea to Miami, licensed the concept to a fitness club and watched it sweep through America and the world.

▓ *The No. 1 Ladies Detective Agency* – my personal favourite, a classic example of a niche business, with Alexander McCall Smith's wonderfully warm and wise creation, Mma Precious Ramotswe, opening her detective agency in downtown

Gaborone, the Botswana capital, and capturing business through being the one and only ladies' detective agency in town – an initial competitive advantage, sustainable in that even if a direct competitor were to emerge, Mma Ramotse's would remain forever the No. 1.

What is your competitive advantage? Is it sustainable?

Essential case study

Extramural Ltd Strategic Review, 2013

Chapter 5: Competitive advantage

Richard and Jane Davies have concluded their analysis of the overall school activity tour market – on demand (Chapter 3) and supply (Chapter 4). They have used the findings of their intern's structured interview programme to help draw up customer purchasing criteria (CPCs) and key success factors (KSFs). Now they use the findings further to help rate Extramural's competitive position – see Table 5.3.

Table 5.3 **Extramural Ltd: competitive position in school activity tours**

Key success factors: school activity tours	Weighting	ActivTours	Extramural	STL
Market share	20%	5	3.4	2.1
Cost factors: Economies of scale, occupancy	25%	4	3.5	3
Management factors: Sales, marketing, CRM	10%	4	5	3
Differentiation factors: Safety and security	10%	5	4.5	4.5
Product quality and range	20%	4.5	4	4
Customer service and delivery	15%	4.5	3	4
Competitive position	**100%**	**4.5**	**3.8**	**3.3**

Key: 1 = Weak, 2 = Tenable, 3 = Favourable, 4 = Strong, 5 = Dominant

The Davieses have mixed feelings over the results. On the one hand, they confirm what they already knew – ActivTours is the market leader, not just in market share but in competitive position and hence profitability. On the other hand, the differential seems high. Sure, Extramural emerges as a favourable to strong player with a rating of 3.8 out of 5 – but with a 15% differential off the leader, which seems uncomfortably high.

The Davieses examine where this differential emanates:

■ *Market share* – no disputing that, it's fact. If ActivTours is allotted a 5 with its market share of 34%, then Extramural's 23% is proportionately a 3.4.

■ *Cost factors* – ActivTours benefits from some economies of scale in purchasing, sales, marketing, especially in advertising, and administration, but occupancy rates during the key peak season are little different, so Extramural's 3.5 to ActivTours' 4 seems reasonable.

■ *Sales and marketing* – Extramural's recognised forte. With their background in the package tour business, the Davieses have run from the outset a highly slick sales and marketing effort, enabling Extramural to keep occupancy rates high as the company expanded in the 1990s and 2000s.

■ *Safety and security* – the Davieses cede leadership to ActivTours here, whose philosophy is to go the extra mile, unnecessarily and expensively in the Davieses' view, given that Extramural's own safety and security systems are first rate.

■ *Product quality and range* – again here Extramural chooses not to compete fully with ActivTours' leadership, whether in introducing state-of-the-art treetop high wire facilities or offering obscure, little-frequented new activities to broaden the range.

■ *Customer service and delivery* – here the Davieses are more concerned. They place great store on satisfying customers, but the survey results are unambiguous – customers are looked after better at ActivTours, and also at STL.

Overall, Extramural rates below ActivTours in every KSF bar one, sales and marketing.

No wonder, the Davieses conclude, somewhat grudgingly, that ActivTours achieves higher margins.

▶

They move on to examine Extramural's competitive position in each product/market segment within their school activity tour business. They find there is not a huge difference, but Extramural emerges better placed among combined learning/activity tours than in pure activity tours – though the company seems less well placed in combined football/activity tours. Extramural is best placed of all in the summer residential camp business, where marketing is crucial, with a 20% KSF weighting, and plays more to Extramural's strengths.

Next they try reviewing Extramural's resources and capabilities in the school activity tour business to see whether any further light can be shed – see Figure 5.4.

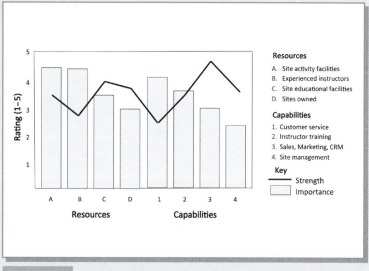

Figure 5.4   **Extramural Ltd: resource and capability assessment**

These findings are even bleaker. They show starkly that Extramural is relatively strong in two capabilities that are of borderline strategic importance:

- Site ownership (resource #3)
- Sales and marketing (capability #1)
- Site management (capability #4).

They also show that the company is relatively weak in two areas which are of great strategic importance:

■ Experienced instructors (resource #3)

■ Customer service (capability #1).

These two analyses provide the Davieses with much food for thought. It is just as well they are not thinking of exiting in the next year or two – a diligent buyer would pick up on these aspects of current *relative* underperformance and that would be reflected in the price offered.

The Davieses have time to put things right and to reach a new level of performance and profitability by their planned time of exit in five years' time. They resolve to do just that – see Chapter 6.

The Davieses repeat these analyses for their two other businesses. They find that competitive position in educational tours and in day camps is much less solid, with Extramural evidently sub-scale in both businesses. We shall return to these two businesses when considering Extramural's corporate strategy in Chapter 8.

Essential checklist on tracking competitive advantage

■ How competitive is your firm in your main business segments? How does your firm rate against its principal competitors?

■ How is that likely to change over time in the absence of this strategy process?

■ Does your firm possess a discernible competitive advantage? Is it sustainable?

■ To answer these important questions, rate your firm's performance against each of the key success factors identified in Chapter 4. Use value chain analysis to gain further insights.

■ How strategically important are your firm's resources and capabilities? Use a comb chart to assess them. What are the strategic implications of your findings?

■ If your business is a start-up in an existing market, be sure you have a distinct competitive advantage to survive, especially in the early stages when competing against established players. If you are creating a new product or service, conduct the basic research to lend credence to your belief that you will find ready buyers, in the right quantities and at the right price.

6

Targeting the strategic gap

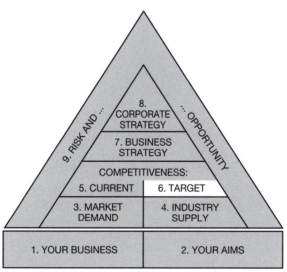

"" We know what we are, but know not what we may be.

William Shakespeare

In this chapter

- Targeting the portfolio gap
- Targeting the capability gap
  - Profiling the ideal player
  - Specifying the target gap
- Targeting the gap in a start-up

In Chapter 5 you assessed your competitive position in each main product/market segment in your business. You pinpointed the source of your competitive advantage in each.

If your firm has more than one business, you did the same for each business.

You have worked out your current competitiveness. Now, where do you want it to be in three to five years' time? What is your target competitiveness?

In this chapter you will identify the strategic gap between where you are now and where the ideal player is, now and in the future. You will then set your sights on the extent to which you aim to narrow, even bridge that gap.

There are two distinct types of gap:

■ In which product/market segments you should compete – the portfolio gap
■ How you will compete in each of those segments – the capability gap.

The portfolio and capability gaps together form the strategic gap. Here you will identify and target the gap. In Chapter 7 you will look at the strategic options for bridging it.

You should assume in Chapters 6 and 7 that you are developing a strategy for a single business, just the one strategic business unit. This is business strategy. In Chapter 8, you will bridge the gap for your portfolio of businesses, through corporate strategy.

Ironically and a bit confusingly, however, the most essential tool in this chapter was designed for purposes of corporate strategy. But the attractiveness/advantage matrix (see Figure 6.1 later) works just as well for – and is essential to – business strategy.

Whether this matrix is used for corporate or business strategy, the axes are the same. The difference comes in the entities analysed and displayed graphically:

■ In corporate strategy, the units are businesses (or 'strategic business units').
■ In business strategy, the units are business segments, specifically product/market segments within a strategic business unit.

This matrix will be your starting point in identifying the strategic gap. It will identify the portfolio gap.

Targeting the portfolio gap

Where should your business compete? In which segments? How can the strategic position of your business be enhanced?

What should your portfolio of business segments look like? What is the gap from today's portfolio?

The attractiveness/advantage matrix should reveal all. It will show how competitive your firm is in segments graded by order of market attractiveness. You should invest ideally in segments where you are strongest and/or which are the most attractive. And you should consider withdrawal from segments where you are weaker and/or which are the least attractive.

And perhaps you should be looking to enter another business segment (or segments) in *more* attractive markets than the ones you currently address? If so, do you have grounds for believing that you would be at least reasonably placed in this new segment? And that you could soon become well placed?

First, you need to define an 'attractive' market segment. This is to some extent sector-specific, and no two strategists will come up with the same list, but over the years I have found these five factors to be both pertinent and relatively measurable:

- Market size – relative to that of other segments, taken from Chapter 3
- Market demand growth – again taken from Chapter 3
- Competitive intensity – taken from Chapter 4 and allowing for barriers to entry and other forces of industry competition
- Industry profitability – average operating margin compared to other segments
- Market risk – cyclicality, volatility (for example, exposure to country risk) – again taken from Chapter 3.

The larger the market and the faster it is growing, the more attractive, other things being equal, is the market. Likewise the greater the industry profitability. But be careful with the other two factors, where the converse applies. The *greater* the competitive intensity and the *greater* the market risk, the *less* attractive is the market.

You could argue that taking even just these five factors is effectively double-counting certain of them. Market demand growth is a major determinant of internal rivalry, itself one of the five forces in competitive intensity, which is the prime driver of industry profitability. market risk may be inversely proportional to industry profitability.

Any list will be unscientific, but it should be instructive. You will have to use your own judgement on the composition of the factors, as well as their weighting. Easiest is to give each of the five an equal weighting, so a rating for overall market attractiveness would be the simple average of the ratings for each factor.

You may, however, be risk averse and attach a higher importance to the market risk factor. In this case, you would derive a weighted average.

An example may help (see Table 6.1). Suppose your business is in four product/market segments and you are contemplating entering a fifth. You rate each of the segments against each of the criteria for market attractiveness. Segment D emerges as the most attractive, followed by new segment E. B is rather unattractive. In assessing overall attractiveness, you have gone for a simple average of the ratings against each factor. You could instead have opted for a weighting system, yielding a weighted average. Or you could, say, have double-counted one of the factors, say risk – more accurate, perhaps, but here you opted for simplicity.

Next you pull out the ratings of competitive position you undertook in the last chapter, for each segment. Now you can draw up the attractiveness/advantage matrix, by placing each segment in the appropriate part of the matrix (see Figure 6.1). Segment A, for example, has a competitive position rating of 4.0 (out of 5) and a market attractiveness rating of 2.8 (also out of 5).

Table 6.1   **Market attractiveness: an example**

Segment	A	B	C	D	E (new)
Market size	3	2	2	3	3
Market growth	1	2	3	5	5
Competitive intensity	2	2	3	4	5
Industry profitability	3	3	4	2	2
Market risk	5	2	4	4	2
Overall attractiveness	**2.8**	**2.2**	**3.2**	**3.6**	**3.4**

Key to rating: 1 = Unattractive, 3 = Reasonably attractive, 5 = Highly attractive [For competitive intensity, remember that the more intense the competition, the *less* attractive the market. Likewise for market risk: the riskier the market, the *less* attractive]

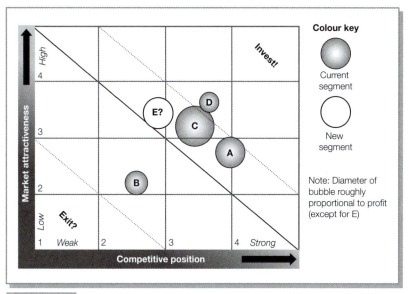

The attractiveness/advantage matrix: an example

The segment's position in the chart will reflect both its competitive position (along the *x*-axis) and its market attractiveness (along the *y*-axis). The size of each circle should be roughly proportional to the segment's contribution to operating profit.

The closer your segment is positioned towards the top right-hand corner the better placed it is. Above the top-right dotted diagonal, you should invest further in that segment, building on your advantage. Should the segment sink below the bottom-left dotted diagonal, however, you should harvest the business for cash or consider withdrawal. Segments placed along the main diagonal are reasonably placed and should be held, with investment cases carefully scrutinised.

The overall strategic position shown in this example seems sound. It shows favourable strength in the biggest and reasonably attractive segment, C, and an excellent position in the somewhat less attractive segment A. Segment D is highly promising and demands more attention, given the currently low level of profit.

Segment B should perhaps be exited – it's a rather unattractive segment, and your firm is not that well placed. The new segment E seems promising.

You may consider the following strategic options worthy of further analysis:

- Holding and steady development in segments A and C
- Investment in segment D
- Entry to segment E (with competitive position improving over time as market share develops)
- Harvesting or exit from segment B.

How is the overall strategic position in your business? Hopefully your *main* segments, from which you derive most revenues, should find themselves positioned above the main diagonal.

Do you have any new segments in mind? How attractive are they? How well placed would you be?

Are there any segments you should be thinking of getting out of? Be careful here, though. Would withdrawal from one segment adversely affect your position in another? Might it be best to persevere with a loss leader?

Which segments are so important that you would derive greatest benefit from improving your competitive position? Where should you concentrate your efforts?

Essential tip

A major criticism of this portfolio planning tool lies in its subjectivity. Some argue that so many judgement calls are made throughout the process that deriving strategy from its findings is fraught with danger.

But strategy is all about judgement, albeit backed up by fact where available. The very process of constructing the matrix, taking in work done throughout Chapters 3–5, is illuminating, instructive and crucial to strategy development. It forces you to think about what drives success in your business, how your business fares against those drivers, and what you need to do to fare better in the future. It is not only a portfolio planning tool but the first step in identifying the strategic gap.

No strategy tools can obviate the need for judgement. Nor should they be expected to.

Targeting the capability gap

Targeting the capability gap is best undertaken in two stages:

■ *Profiling the ideal player* – identifying the maximum gap
■ *Specifying the target gap* – setting your sights on the target gap.

Start by considering the ideal player, the perfect provider of the goods and services also provided by your firm.

Profiling the ideal player

What will perfection look like in your business?

That may not be you, nor may you choose for it to be so. But it can be instructive to think about what that ideal player will look like in three to five years' time.

You have decided in which product/market segments you will compete over the next five years. Here, and in the next tool, you target how you choose to compete in those segments.

First you profile the ideal player. There are three stages in this process:

■ Envisioning future scenarios
■ Assessing key success factors in each scenario
■ Identifying common capabilities.

You will envision the future marketplace and the players therein. You will build scenarios about the future and consider what would be the capabilities of the ideal player under each scenario. Then you can deduce what capabilities are common to these players in all or most of the scenarios. These could become the minimum target capabilities for you to aim for.

Envisioning future scenarios

Here you need to envision the future of your marketplace. Will it be more competitive? Will customers have different expectations? Will players need to develop different capabilities?

To answer these questions, it may help to do some brainstorming, thinking a bit more creatively and laterally than you may have done this far in Chapters 3 to 5. You need to go through and beyond what you have done earlier.

Brainstorming is a structured process for the generation of ideas. It can be done individually or in a group setting.

For the individual brainstorming is different strokes for different folks. I like to brainstorm while walking – preferably on a clifftop above the Cambrian Sea, with jagged rocks and swooping cormorants to one side and lush pastures and baaing sheep to the other. Others find inspiration in yoga or the flotation tank.

In the corporate setting, it works best if you escape from your place of work, perhaps to a country house setting, with brainstorming in the morning, group activities such as archery or improvised drama in the early afternoon, followed by more brainstorming and wrapping-up in the late afternoon.

The idea is to try to get people to think 'out of the box', using the imagination, stimulating the right side of the brain. Encourage plenty of use of visuals, whether through projectors, flipcharts or Post-it notes.

Try to develop a range of scenarios on what may happen in your marketplace. Venture beyond the more likely outcomes – you've already drawn those up. Think of those that are less expected but still *quite* likely to occur. Stay clear of fanciful outcomes with only a remote chance of happening. Go for scenarios that could actually happen.

Apply the reasonability test: 'Is it reasonable for me to assume that such and such an outcome could take place over the next five years? Sure, it may be less likely to happen than the other outcome, but looking back five years from now would I be surprised that it actually happened?'

Settle on *two to four scenarios*. Give each a name, something that brings the scenario to life.

Assessing key success factors in each scenario

You assessed the key success factors (KSFs) required to meet the needs of customers in Chapter 4. Now you should consider what KSFs are required to meet possibly amended future customer needs, under each of the scenarios you have envisioned.

Some KSFs may become more important in one scenario, with therefore a higher weighting. The converse may be true for other KSFs.

Some KSFs may become more important in one scenario, but less important in another. Some KSFs may be brand new.

Draw up the amended and re-weighted KSFs for each scenario. The ideal player in that scenario will be the company with the highest achievable rating against each of the KSFs.

You should do this for each of the two to four scenarios you have brainstormed.

Identifying common capabilities

The final step in envisioning the ideal player is to investigate what capabilities are common in each of the scenarios.

Some will be pertinent to only one scenario, others to more than one. One or two may be applicable to all scenarios.

You mustn't forget here your original, most likely scenario, the KSFs developed in Chapter 4. Those that were identified and weighted there remain the most important, since they are the ones most likely to be needed. These you are now adding or reconsidering may represent just the icing on the cake.

Lack of commonality doesn't necessarily mean that isolated KSFs are unimportant. But it does mean that, in the next tool, you may choose not to take a particular KSF into account. You won't have the time or resources to prepare for every eventuality. Choices will have to be made. In the words of Michael Porter, 'strategy is about making choices, trade-offs; it's about deliberately choosing to be different'.

If one or two KSFs are common to most, even all, scenarios, they could become target capabilities on which you can set your sights.

You're drawing a picture of the ideal player in your marketplace over the next few years. Next you'll judge to what extent you should aim to acquire the capabilities of the ideal player.

Essential tip

Be careful to keep your feet on the ground. Brainstorming workshops need firm direction, or venturing into the realms of fantasy may prove too tempting. The scenarios must be plausible. There is no point in considering the KSFs needed for a scenario which has a miniscule chance of happening – although you may need to think about how your firm would survive in a 'Black Swan' event (see Chapter 9).

Specifying the target gap

How close to perfection should you aim?

You have envisioned the ideal player in your marketplace in three to five years' time. You identified the capabilities needed for competing perfectly in the future.

Now you need to identify the gap between your firm's capabilities now and those to which you aspire. It asks you to reconsider where you aim to be. Are you sure you've set sufficiently challenging goals?

Should you be stretching your sights and making your plans more ambitious? Should you aim to become the ideal player in your type of service? Should you be 'going for goal'?

You then revisit your assessment of competitive position in Chapter 5 in the light of the scenarios you've developed and your newly reset sights. And you identify the shortfall between your current capabilities and those to which you aspire.

This is the capability gap. In Chapter 7, you'll select a strategy on how to bridge this gap.

There are three steps in specifying the target gap:

1 Stretching your sights
2 Aiming towards the ideal player
3 Identifying the capability gap.

Stretching your sights

Where do you want your business to be in five years' time? What vision of your firm did you create in Chapter 2? Do you envision doing more or less what you are doing today, serving more or less the same customers, but better?

That's fine. If, however, your firm has greater ambitions, you may want to raise those sights. How about raising the bar on your firm's aspirations? How about raising the return on capital?

How close to the ideal player should you aim to become in your product/market segments of choice?

Aiming towards the ideal player

In Chapter 5 you identified your firm's strengths and weaknesses and rated them against the key success factors (KSFs) required to compete in each of your main business segments. You found that there was a gap between your firm's overall rating and that of the ideal player, who realistically would have gained a rating of between 4 and 5 (out of 5) against each KSF.

In this last chapter, you have envisioned scenarios where new KSFs

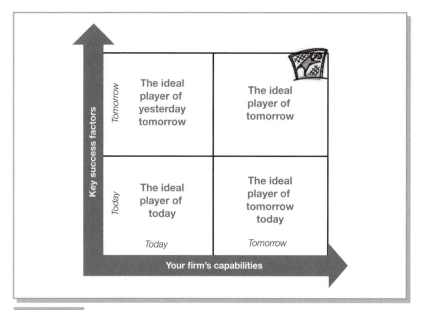

Figure 6.2   **Going for goal**

may be required or existing KSFs gain in prominence. These could further widen the KSF gap – if you were to sit still.

Where do you want to be in tomorrow's marketplace? Do you want to become a good player in tomorrow's marketplace? A strong player?

Or do you want to *lead* in tomorrow's marketplace?

Do you want to get as far as you can towards becoming the Ideal Player of Tomorrow? Do you want to 'go for goal'? – see a chart I developed recently for a client in Figure 6.2.

If so, however, remember that the goalposts may well have shifted by the time you're ready to shoot. Time moves on, and the ideal player in five years' time will have a different mix of capabilities from the equivalent today – perhaps only with slight differences in nuance, perhaps radically different.

The *Going for goal* chart highlights three important points:

■ It's fine being the *ideal player of today*, but today lasts only one day.

■ If your firm doesn't develop the extra capabilities required to meet the customer needs of tomorrow, you'll become the *ideal player of yesterday tomorrow*.

■ There's little point in developing extra capabilities today unless customers need them, or you'll become the *ideal player of tomorrow today.*

Once you've raised your sights, perhaps to the very top, you need to specify the capability gap and, in the next chapter, plan how you are going to bridge it.

Identifying the capability gap

In Chapter 5, you set out your ratings against the KSFs you derived in Chapter 4 for each of your main business segments. These KSFs were in turn largely based on customer needs you identified and ranked earlier.

That assessment was not a purely static exercise. You were encouraged to take a dynamic perspective. You looked not just at customer needs and KSFs today, but how they might change over the next few years. You also considered how your firm might improve its standing against one or more of the KSFs over the next few years. *And* you gave some thought as to how your competitors might enhance *their* standing in the future.

You need to revisit those charts. You should check for any changes in customer needs, KSFs, your firm's competitive position, or that of a competitor, as a result of changes in:

■ The external marketplace, given the scenario development you have undertaken above

■ Your goals, given any resetting of your sights.

You can now identify the capability gap. You've revisited your competitive position in each of your main business segments and established to what extent there is a gap in each KSF with the ideal player.

You now target that gap. Often that means just the insertion of an active verb, such as 'improve'. Suppose you have in one of your segments an ineffective distribution system – targeting that gap means improving distribution.

Sometimes targeting the gap requires further thought. The capability gap may be too broad and you should consider exiting the segment.

Let's return to the example we used earlier in this chapter of the business operating in four main segments and contemplating entry to a fifth. As a result of profiling the ideal player and raising sights as above, the strategist may now target the capability gap as follows:

■ Improving margin in segment A

■ Withdrawing in segment B, recognising an unbridgeable gap

■ Improving distribution in segment C

■ Improving product speed to market in segment D

■ Entering segment E

■ Lowering production costs across all segments

■ Improving enterprise resource management ('ERM') systems across the business.

The resultant impact of this targeting of the capability gap could be as shown in Figure 6.3. The competitive position of each segment, especially E, should be improved, other than B, which will be exited. The overall strategic position of this business could be greatly improved.

Note that targeting the capability gap does not at this stage specify the *means* of bridging it. That is left for the discussion on strategic options in Chapter 7.

Improving distribution is a capability gap in segment C. Switching to a new distributor would be a strategic option.

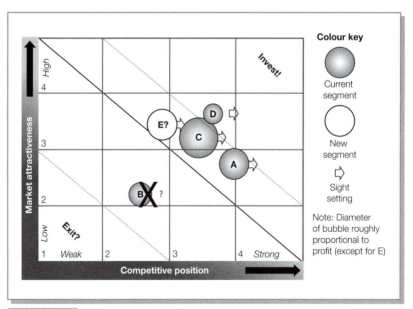

Figure 6.3 Strategic repositioning: an example

Lowering production costs across all segments is a capability gap. Outsourcing or offshoring would be a strategic option.

Essential example

Could Liverpool FC be champions again?

Not just down, but well and truly out at half-time, the football world nodded its collective head. Liverpool were lucky even to be there in the 2005 Champions League final, having scraped past Juventus and Chelsea in earlier rounds, and had no right to be playing on the same turf as the majestic Milan.

The likes of Pirlo, Shevchenko and Kaká had mercilessly exposed the gulf in class between the two teams, running in three classy first-half goals.

But Liverpool dug on their reserves of Scouser grit and fought back to 3–3 at full time. Following a dramatic penalty shoot-out, the trophy was held aloft by Liverpudlians for the fifth time – and now rests forever in a cabinet at Anfield HQ.

But can there ever be a sixth?

Football has become big business. Driven by satellite, cable and pay TV revenues on the one hand, and by product endorsements on the other, top footballers now earn as much as pop stars or bankers. They are affordable only by the big or the rich.

To be big, a club needs a large, all-seater stadium, with top-notch corporate hospitality facilities – like Manchester United's Old Trafford or Arsenal's Emirates, though even these are dwarfed by the 100,000 capacity of Barcelona's Camp Nou.

To be rich, a club needs a sugar daddy – like at Chelsea, Manchester City or Paris St Germain.

To be quite big and quite rich, like Liverpool, can mean, at best, occasional success. Liverpool's average attendance at Anfield of around 45,000 compares to Manchester United's 75,000 and Arsenal's 60,000. It is of the same order of magnitude as for Manchester City and Chelsea, but they have their sugar daddies.

On average attendance alone, it is fairer to compare Liverpool's recent modest league record with that of Newcastle United (50,000) or Sunderland (40,000). Liverpool's Champions League exploits of 2005–08 take on a different complexion.

Clubs like Liverpool can invest heavily in the occasional world-class player, like Steven Gerrard, Fernando Torres or Luis Suárez, but not 11 or more of them, like Chelsea or Manchester City.

Like most football clubs, Liverpool is run as a genuine business. Its owners may be self-made millionaires, in this case American, but their goal is to maximise shareholder value, hence capital gain upon exit. Liverpool is not run as a plaything for the obscenely rich.

This means that Liverpool can ill afford to make costly mistakes – and there have been a few of those in recent years. One such was the purchase of the raw Andy Carroll for £35m, after the sale of Fernando Torres for £50m. Former manager Kenny Dalglish's subsequent comment that Carroll 'cost us minus 15 million pounds' must go down as one of the managerial howlers of business history.

With another new manager and less money in the bank, what is the strategic gap Liverpool FC now needs to target? At first sight, the answer might seem quite obvious. Liverpool must either extend its stadium capacity by at least one-third, or find a sugar daddy.

But such a conclusion may be premature. This book recommends a nine-step strategy development process, the Strategy Pyramid. And in step 4 in particular, industry analysis, things are changing. UEFA has issued a set of financial fair play ('FFP') rules to develop a more level playing field (literally) between the top clubs.

UEFA wants each club to run its affairs as a proper business, not as an oligarch's toy. Operating losses, with appropriate amortisation rates for capital expenditure on transfer fees, are being monitored and controlled. Limits have been set and clubs that exceed them will be penalised, with a graded series of disciplinary measures, ranging from warnings, reprimands and fines to points deductions and even elimination from the Champions League.

FFP is admirable in principle. In practice there will be difficulties – the super-wealthy clubs will seek ways to dodge it. Manchester City and Paris St Germain have arranged massive sponsorship deals with owners' companies, ostensibly for stadium and shirt naming rights, in effect displacing former direct loans or grants. But UEFA is unbowed and has stated that it will not permit the wealthy clubs to cheat. This is all good news for the lawyers.

Hopefully, clubs will be able to target the strategic gap from a more commercial perspective. In the case of Liverpool, that means looking dispassionately at how the club rates today against the key success factors (KSFs) of the football industry, how the ideal club of tomorrow would rate and to what extent Liverpool should aim to bridge that gap.

Liverpool's targeting the strategic gap might include, against these KSFs:

■ Cost factors:

  – *Stadium capacity* – extend by one-third, possibly sharing a new stadium in Stanley Park with local rivals, Everton FC

  – *Player remuneration* – take time, don't be rushed into transfers or new contracts

  – *Academy* – improve conversion rate of young players into the first team, as at Barcelona.

■ Management factors:

  – Have faith, think Manchester United or Arsenal managerial longevity rather than the soap opera that is Chelsea.

■ Differentiation factors:

  – *Product quality* – rebuild squad steadily and cost-effectively; go for a Mishu rather than a Carroll, improve team interplay, preferably Barcelona-style

  – *Passion* – Liverpool is peerless at the nostalgia factor, comparable only to the Welsh rugby team

  – *Marketing* – compete with Manchester United for the global market, especially in Asia, with pre-season tours

  – *Service* – spoil the supporters, improve loyalty schemes, put on special shows.

The football world was right. Liverpool outperformed its resources and capabilities in the football industry of 2005–08, largely due to passion-fuelled commitment and inspiration.

But in the new world of FFP, Liverpool, along with other clubs with passionate local support underpinning their every endeavour, from Newcastle to Swansea, Aston Villa to West Ham, can plan their renaissance. With UEFA behind them, they will never walk alone.

Targeting the gap in a start-up

In Chapter 5, we concluded that the secret to a successful start-up is to hit the ground running with an evident competitive advantage.

But how defensible is that advantage?

If your new venture succeeds, you will be targeted. Competitors will eye your newly carved space with envy. They will come after you. And soon.

Remember the definition we used for strategy: strategy is how a company deploys its scarce resources to gain a sustainable advantage over the competition. The all-important word for a start-up is *sustainable*.

How will you protect yourself against the inevitable competitive response? There are a number of ways you can try to sustain your competitive advantage:

- Patent protection of key products
- Sustained innovation, staying one step ahead in product development
- Sustained process improvement, staying one step ahead in cost competitiveness and efficiency
- Investment in branding, identifying in the mind of the customer the particular benefit brought by your offering with its name
- Investment, for business-to-business ventures, in customer relationships.

The process for determining your strategy to counteract competitive response, however, is the same as for an established business above.

In profiling the ideal player, you should include in your envisioning a scenario where there is a ferocious competitive response to your presence from the competitor, direct or indirect, you most fear.

In specifying the target gap, you must go for goal – becoming the ideal player in your chosen niche market.

You must identify the capability gap between where you will be at launch and where the ideal player will be three to five years hence.

That is the gap you will target. Nothing less will do. The vast majority of new businesses fail in the first five years. You either eat or are eaten. You have to go for it, go for goal.

In the next chapter we shall look at how your new venture will set out to bridge the capability gap and sustain its competitive advantage.

Footnote: strategic gap analysis has its critics, with two perceived shortcomings:

■ Rectifying weaknesses may be less value enhancing than building on strengths.

■ Capabilities are not as easily developed as resources.

The first point is important. Your competitive position may be favourable in a segment, but investment to upgrade that position towards that of the ideal player may be costly – and unviable. The financial rate of return on the investment may be below the opportunity cost of investing in another segment or business-wide project.

This does not negate the validity of the approach. It merely emphasises that the strategic options to bridge that gap need to be thoroughly analysed, in commercial and financial terms, in Chapter 7.

The second point relates to the difference between resources and capabilities. Football teams with huge resources are frequently outplayed by those with a fraction of those resources but with superior performance capabilities on the day. Do you recall, as I do with glee, as a Liverpool supporter, 7th November 2006 and Southend United 1 Manchester United 0?!

Success tends to lie with organisations which possess capabilities that best leverage their resources. These capabilities are not easily developed. Creating them organically can be a lengthy and difficult process and may best be acquired through acquisition or alliance. Either way can be expensive. And success in developing capabilities, unlike in deploying resources, cannot be guaranteed.

Thus, in the example of Figure 6.3, targeting the capability gap in segment D through improving product speed to market sounds easy enough, but in reality might be a lengthy, expensive, complex, management-intensive challenge.

Again, this critique does not negate the tool, but it stresses that gap analysis is but an intermediate tool in the process of developing a commercially and financially viable strategy.

Essential tip

Strategic gap analysis has its critics. Capabilities, they say, are not as easily developed as resources. And rectifying weaknesses may be less value enhancing than building on strengths. These are perfectly valid points – but use gap analysis, nevertheless, along with your common sense.

Essential case study

Extramural Ltd Strategic Review, 2013

Chapter 6: The strategic gap

Richard and Jane Davies have been looking forward to this sixth step in the strategy process. They formed their business over 20 years ago and are proud of their creation. But they recognise that not everything has gone right. Sometimes they have planned carefully and things have worked out well. At other times they have reacted opportunistically, with varying degrees of success.

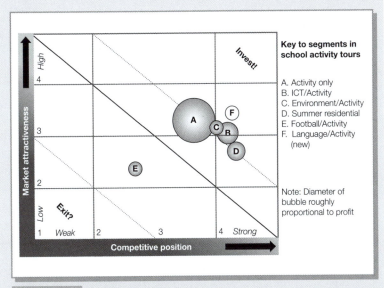

| Figure 6.4 | Extramural Ltd: strategic position in school activity tours |

Here is their chance to lay the foundation for where they want their company to be in five years' time, when they intend to bow out.

They start with the school activity tour business and ask themselves in which product/market segments they should compete over the next five years. Having already assessed in Chapter 5 their relative competitiveness in each of these segments, they quickly draw up an attractiveness/advantage matrix (see Figure 6.4).

This shows immediately that Extramural's strategic position in this business is sound – they have favourable to strong positions in segments that are in the main attractive. The new language/activity tour segment seems the most promising, with summer residential camps less so despite the segment's faster growth, due to its relatively low occupancy and profitability.

The exception is football/activity tours. Dominated by one long-established specialist player, Footie4Kids, Extramural's position is tenable but the market is the least attractive of all. Unless they can find strong links and synergies with other segments, the Davieses may need to consider withdrawal from this segment.

Armed with this portfolio backdrop, the Davieses embark on profiling the ideal player in this market over the next five years. To get them into the right frame of mind for brainstorming, they jump into the car and take the 45-minute drive to Totnes, site of their first-ever activity centre (long since abandoned, after it proved too small). There they hire a chunky 15-foot cabin cruiser and set off on a one-day chug down and back up the River Dart, taking in the springtime flora of the verdant Dart valley along the way.

They moor at a riverside inn midway to Dartmouth, treat themselves to some homemade steak pie, washed down by the local 'Proper Ansome' ale, retire to the river garden, let their minds drift freely between issues of market demand, competition and customer needs, and come up with three scenarios, each worthy of consideration in their strategy development process:

■ *Picky!* – customers get increasingly demanding – on product quality, range and service – as peak season supply expands to meet current excess demand.

■ *Aggro!* – Market leader ActivTours opts to maximise
  occupancy by lowering off-peak prices.

■ *Nightmare!* – a child is seriously injured while undertaking a
  licensed activity at a licensed centre.

Each of the first two is at least reasonably likely to occur and
Extramural needs a strategy that can cope. The third, they pray,
is highly unlikely, given the safety systems put into place by all
licensed operators, but the nightmare could conceivably happen.

So what of the ideal player under these scenarios? The Davieses
figure that the ideal player will need full competence in these
KSFs over and above those set out in Chapter 5:

■ *Picky!* – weighting for the product quality, product range and
  customer service KSFs will become higher and the ideal player
  will have to invest in facilities, systems and customer service
  to meet tougher customer demands and retain top rating
  against each of these KSFs.

■ *Aggro!* – the ideal player will need to retain custom and margin
  through either cutting back on off-peak variable costs or
  firming up a niche offering which will prove resilient to a price
  battle.

■ *Nightmare!* – the ideal player will not only have safety facilities
  and systems second to none but be recognised as such in the
  market to survive the inevitable market contraction that would
  follow such a scenario.

The Davieses don't at first see much commonality between the
KSFs needed for each of the three scenarios. But gradually a
picture emerges. The ideal player must be highly rated (defined
as at least 4 out of 5) against KSFs such as product quality/range
and safety/security, but should also possess a niche offering
of undisputed excellence to be able to differentiate itself in the
market and give some protection against tougher times.

The Davieses chug on downriver towards Dartmouth, debating
ways and means of bridging the gap – but that is for Chapter 7.

Essential checklist on targeting the strategic gap

You have worked out how well placed you are in each of your main addressed business segments.

In this chapter you target the gap between where you are now and where you want to be in three to five years' time.

First you target the portfolio gap. Use the attractiveness/advantage tool to chart your target strategic position of the future.

Next you target the capability gap. This you do in two stages:

- Profiling the ideal player
    - Envisioning future scenarios
    - Assessing key success factors in each scenario
    - Identifying common capabilities.
- Specifying the target gap
    - Stretching your sights
    - Aiming towards the ideal player – and maybe going for goal
    - Identifying the capability gap.

The output is a set of target capability gaps, the bridging of which can be accomplished by a range of strategic options and is the focus of the next chapter.

If yours is a start-up business, how defensible is your initial competitive advantage? How can you protect yourself against competitive response? What is the capability gap between where you are now and where you need to be to be protected?

7

Bridging the gap: business strategy

> **"** Don't be afraid to take a big step. You can't cross a chasm in two short jumps.
>
> *David Lloyd George*

In this chapter

- ▓ Opting for a generic strategy
  - – Essential tool: The experience curve

■ Strategic repositioning and shaping profit growth options
 – Essential tool: Uncontested market space

■ Making the strategic investment decision

■ Bridging the gap for a start-up

■ Business strategic risks and opportunities

In the last chapter you identified and targeted the capability gap. If yours is a multi-business company, you did that for each business.

Now you need to bridge the strategic gap. This has three distinct but interrelated aspects:

■ Bridging the capability gap in each business

■ Optimising your business portfolio

■ Leveraging your resources.

The latter two aspects belong to corporate strategy, which we deal with in the next chapter. The first is business strategy and we tackle that here.

Opting for a generic strategy

Michael Porter's three generic, business-level strategies have been with us since the early 1980s and still form the base camp from which strategists ascend to the peak. They are strategies (see Figure 7.1) of:

■ Cost leadership

■ Differentiation

■ Focus.

Any one of these strategies can yield sustainable competitive advantage. Pursue two or all three of these strategies in the same

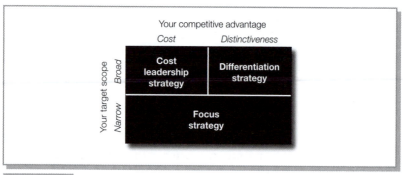

Figure 7.1 **Three generic strategies**

Source: Adapted from Porter, M.E., *Competitive Strategy: Techniques for Analzying Industries and Competitors* (The Free Press, 2004)

business and you will in all probability end up 'stuck in the middle' – a recipe for long-term under-performance.

What is the primary source of competitive advantage in your business? Is it cost? Or is it the distinctiveness of your product and/or service offering?

Think back on Chapter 5, where you rated your business in its key product/market segments against your industry's key success factors (KSFs). Did your business get higher ratings against the cost KSFs or the differentiation KSFs?

And go back one stage further. In Chapter 4 you identified and weighted KSFs in each key segment. Did you give a higher weighting to differentiation factors than to cost factors? Or the other way round?

There is little to be gained in being a cost leader in a segment which is not price sensitive, likewise in being a highly differentiated producer in a segment where customers perceive little differentiation and demand only least cost.

If cost factors are most important in your business and you rated well or at least promisingly against them, then you should opt for a strategy of cost leadership.

If differentiating factors are more important and you rated well or at least promisingly against them, you should pursue a strategy of differentiation.

Either strategy can yield a sustainable competitive advantage. Either you supply a product that is at lower cost than those of your competitors, or you supply a product that is sufficiently differentiated from those of your competitors that customers are prepared to pay a premium price – where the incremental price charged adequately covers the incremental costs of supplying the differentiated product.

For a ready example of a successful low-cost strategy, think of Southwest Airlines, easyJet or Air Asia, where relentless maximisation of load factor enables them to offer seats at scarcely credible prices compared with those that prevailed before they entered the scene. And they still produce a profit. Or think of IKEA's stylish but highly price-competitive furniture.

A classic example of the differentiation strategy is Apple – never the cheapest, whether in PCs, laptops or mobile phones, but always stylistically distinctive and feature-intensive. Or Prêt-à-Manger in fresh, high-quality fast food.

These two strategies were long recognised before Porter introduced his generic strategies. He identified a third, the focus strategy. While acknowledging that a firm can typically prosper in its industry by following either a low-cost or a differentiation strategy, one alternative is not to address the whole industry but to narrow the scope and focus on a slice of it, a single segment.

Under these circumstances, a firm can achieve market leadership through focused differentiation leading over time to scale and experience-driven low unit costs (see the text box on the experience curve) compared to less focused players in that segment.

The classic example of a successful focus strategy is Honda motorcycles, whose focus on product reliability over decades yielded the global scale to enable its differentiated, quality products to become and remain cost competitive.

Be aware, though, that any generic strategy is vulnerable to shifting customer needs and preferences. No strategy should be set in stone.

If you pursue a low-cost strategy, beware of a shift in customer needs putting a greater emphasis on quality, for which customers are prepared to pay a higher price. An example is the cinema industry. For years many chains followed a policy of shoving the customers into their 'flea pits', keeping costs down to a minimum. Customers deserted in droves, opting for the comfort of their living rooms and the ease of the video recorder. Today some cinemas offer reclining seats and waiter service – the diametrically opposite concept to the flea pit, and a service many customers are happy to pay for.

Likewise, if you pursue a strategy of differentiation, beware of changing customer preferences. Customers may be prepared to shift to a new entrant offering a product or service of markedly inferior quality to yours, but good enough and at a significant price discount. The classic example is that of low-cost airlines, originating in the US and spreading rapidly to the UK, Europe and Asia, and forcing the full-service national carriers to radically rethink their business model.

The canny business will spot the emergent trend and open a new business, preferably under a new brand, so as not to blur the image of the brand in the eyes of the customer. They will pursue one generic strategy in one business and a different one in another.

There is, however, no guarantee of success in the new business, given that it will operate in an entirely different culture – viz. the short-lived airline Go, launched by British Airways to address the booming low-cost market and eventually swallowed by easyJet itself. Likewise, attempts by Ford Motor Company to move into more differentiated businesses via acquisition proved not to be value enhancing and the Jaguar and Land Rover divisions were soon sold on.

But it is especially inadvisable to mix strategies in one business, even if you are doing so in different segments. By definition, a strategic business unit operates in product/market segments that are interrelated – whether by offering the same or similar products or services or addressing the same or similar customer groups. One strategy in one segment coupled with another strategy in another segment can not only confuse the customer but again land you 'stuck in the middle'.

Essential tip

Go for one of the main generic strategies or the other – low-cost or differentiation. Don't do what so many companies do and go for both. They end up stuck in the middle of the road and getting run over.

Essential tool

The experience curve

One of the three generic, business-level strategies, the focus strategy, displays elements of both the differentiation and low-cost strategies. This is largely due to the effects of the 'experience curve' – a concept most important to business success.

The concept as we know it today was developed by The Boston Consulting Group in the 1960s. In a series of studies on a broad range of industries, from beer and toilet paper to machinery and industrial components, BCG found that the unit cost of value added to a standard product declines by a constant percentage (typically between 20 and 30%) each time cumulative output doubles.

BCG ascribed to their 'law of experience' a series of causes, in particular:

■ *Labour efficiency* – workers learn the tricks of the trade, what works, what doesn't, what short-cuts to take – and managers too.

■ *Process efficiency* – processes become optimised and more standardised.

■ *Technology efficiency* – process automation displaces labour inputs.

BCG's research was broad and comprehensive, but not new. Where they broke new ground came in their interpretation of the research and its implications for strategy. If the player with the largest cumulative experience would have the lowest unit costs of production, then strategy should be aimed at maximising sales and production, hence market share, rather than maximising profit.

This was the theoretical underpinning of BCG's growth share matrix (see Chapter 8). Due to the experience curve, relative market share should be a firm indicator of relative cost position.

This suggests that one strategic option you should consider is investing heavily in market share gain in a segment where you already have a high market share – and are preferably the market leader.

By gaining further market share, to what extent will the experience curve effect enable you to further reduce unit costs? If this were to be translated into reduced pricing rather than increased margin, what effect would that have on your competitors?

Would they retaliate? Could they also reduce costs through shared experience, for example by poaching one of your employees? Could your strategy force some of the weaker competitors to withdraw from the segment?

It is an ambitious, aggressive strategic option.

Strategic repositioning and shaping profit growth options

You have set your generic strategy. What next?

You need to develop a series of profit growth options consistent with that strategy to bridge the strategic gap identified in Chapter 6.

In that chapter you applied the attractiveness/advantage matrix to your business and concluded that you should invest in certain product/market segments, hold in others and perhaps exit one or two – and, conversely, perhaps enter one or two new ones.

You also targeted the capability gap that needs to be bridged for your firm to achieve your target level of competitiveness in selected segments.

Now you will determine how to bridge the capability gap with profit growth options in each key segment to be invested in. Likewise for segments to be held – and even those to be exited. And you will consider the business as a whole and how it can be reshaped in line with your strategy to generate sustained profit growth.

Finally, you will differentiate between actions you can take now to increase profit in the short term (the next 12 months) and those which will improve strategic position and grow profits in the long term.

Having drawn up a range of profit growth options, you will evaluate them to decide which investment alternatives will yield the greatest return towards the goals and objectives of your firm.

Start by taking one product/market segment at a time. Take those segments you have marked out for investing in, and then move on to those for holding, exit and entry. Finally, look at profit growth options which apply to all segments.

Segments for investment

Take your largest segment, the one that yields the greatest contribution to overhead.

You have already identified the capability gap in this segment. What are the options for bridging it?

The gap may be in new product speed to market. Bridging it may require streamlined processes. You may need to invest in expert advisers.

The gap may be in product reliability. Bridging it may require investment in new equipment, in both production and testing.

The gap may be in customer service. Bridging it may require investment in staff and training, even a cultural shift, achievable only through a controlled change management programme.

In each of these examples, bridging the capability gap is a long-term process. That is often the case, but some profit growth options have faster results.

Indeed, you should actively be on the lookout for short-term profit growth options. There is nothing like a quick win or two following a strategy development process to gladden the boss's heart, justify the investment in time and energy and build team morale.

The quick win could come from a new angle in marketing, in its broadest sense – product, promotion, place, price – revealed in the strategy development process.

One such angle could be to lower prices. But that would reduce profit, not grow it, you might think. Perhaps, but maybe not for long:

- Volumes sold should increase, depending on the sensitivity (or technically 'price elasticity') of demand for the product, holding or growing revenue.

- Market share will be gained, enhancing your presence in the market and potentially stimulating further volume growth.

- Economies of scale may kick in, lowering your unit costs and restoring your operating margin (and even your gross margin, if

Table 7.1 Strategic repositioning and profit growth options

Strategic repositioning	Profit growth options to bridge strategic gap	
	Short-term	Long-term
Segments for investment	• Marketing • Lower pricing to gain share?	Bridge capability gap, invest in: • Fixed and current assets • Business processes • Staff & training
Segments to hold	• Reduce variable cost • Tweak pricing?	• Reduce variable cost • Recompete? • Alliance?
New segments	• Prepare project plan	• Leverage strengths
Segments to exit	• Improve financials?	• Withdraw (sell?)
Whole business	• Benchmark overhead • Marketing	• Reduce overhead • BPR, outsourcing etc. • Resource-based investment

your greater volumes enable you to drive down the unit costs of bought-in materials, components and sub-assemblies).

These are some of the profit growth options, both short and long term, for bridging the capability gap in segments you will invest in. They are summarised in Table 7.1.

Next you consider the profit growth options for those segments which you have chosen for holding – probably not to invest in, but definitely not to withdraw from.

Segments for holding

Holding on in a segment does not mean doing nothing, taking no strategic action. You need to actively manage your segment position and preferably strengthen it.

In the long term there are three profit growth options you should consider:

- *Reduce variable cost.* If you stand still on cost, you run the risk of a competitor undercutting you over time; an ongoing programme of cost reduction would be wise, whether in purchasing or operational efficiency.
- *Recompete.* Change the rules of the game in some way, so that you effectively create a new segment out of the old. Easier said than done, but it has been done again and again – think of a specialist retailer like Pets at Home, which has stolen share from traditional pet shops, supermarkets and DIY chains through offering not just a vast range of pet supplies but a destination in itself, with its rabbit, guinea pig and tropical fish displays captivating customers young and old; or in manufacturing, look for inspiration to the iPhone, so much more than a mere mobile phone.
- *Alliance.* You have a favourable competitive position in a segment which is moderately attractive; perhaps by allying with a competitor you could jointly have a stronger position in that segment and enable superior profit growth prospects for both parties.

In the short term there are other options for you to consider. Cost reduction is both a short- and a long-term option, but you may also consider tweaking your pricing in the segment, whether up or down:

- Nudging pricing up may change customer perceptions and give the impression that you are a premium player, though again you should think carefully on the price elasticity of demand.

There are many examples of this strategy, such as the plethora of 'premium' lager brands in the UK, in reality 'bog standard', mass-market beers in their home countries of Belgium, Germany, France, Italy, Mexico, Singapore, China – the list is endless, with so many playing the same game.

■ Nudging pricing down, again depending on price elasticity, may gain you some extra volume and share, but beware of competitive retaliation.

Segments for exit

Profit growth options in those segments you have chosen to exit is limited. In corporate, as distinct from business, strategy, exiting a business unit can generate value through a structured sale process, including preparing the business for sale ('dressing the bride') and improving the financials pre-sale. In business strategy, your presence in the business segments you choose to exit may have no sale value.

But there may be elements of value in that segment that can find a buyer. There may be some physical assets to sell or even some intangibles such as use of the brand name in that segment.

Segments for entry

In Chapter 6 you identified new segments your firm should consider entering. These should be segments where you can leverage your existing strengths.

The new product/market segment should preferably be synergistic with your existing business, having one or more of these characteristics:

■ It is a new product (or service) related to your existing products and sold to the same customer group.

■ It is the same product and sold to a related customer group.

■ (If it is both a new product *and* to a new customer group, that is highly risky and would require a much tougher degree of substantiation.)

■ It is a segment where key success factors, in both cost and differentiation, mirror the relative strengths of your business.

■ It is one in which some of your direct competitors are prospering and so might you.

■ It is one in which some players in other countries are prospering and there seems no reason why the same should not apply in your country.

In the short term, there is little you can do to improve profit, other than prepare a robust project plan for new segment entry and improve the odds on securing long-term profit growth.

All segments

Finally, you need to consider profit growth options that apply across all segments in your business. Long-term options may include:

■ Reducing overhead costs, having benchmarked them against your competitors in the short term.

■ Improving key business processes, perhaps through redesigning them.

■ Outsourcing, perhaps even offshoring, business processes such as IT, technical support and customer services.

■ Investing in the core competences of your business, whether they be in R&D, operations or sales – see resource-based strategy in Chapter 8.

■ Marketing – leveraging the name of your business across all segments, which is also a potential profit growth option in the short term.

Strategic alternatives

By now you should have a whole range of profit growth options. The danger is that it may look like a laundry list.

It should help to group them into two or three strategic alternatives. Each will represent a defined and coherent strategy for bridging the strategic gap in this business. One alternative may reflect investment primarily in one segment; another may reflect investment spread across a combination of segments and business-wide processes.

They should be mutually exclusive – you can follow one or another, but not both (or all). You can follow just the one alternative.

Grouping into strategic alternatives makes evaluation more manageable. Rather than evaluating 20 profit growth options, you will be evaluating two or three strategic alternatives.

Essential tip

Take care when drawing up profit growth options. The list should not get out of control.

Each option should satisfy two fundamental criteria:

- It should be consistent with your strategy.
- It should seem like a sound investment in itself.

Grouping the options into strategic alternatives further helps manage the process.

Essential tool

Uncontested market space

One of the criticisms long aimed at Michael Porter's five forces industry analysis (see Chapter 4) is that it is too confined, too narrow in focus. The delineation of industry boundaries for analysis of the five forces and the shaping of a competitive strategy within that industry may constrict the strategist so rigidly that the opportunity for genuine value innovation beyond current industry boundaries may be lost.

Two INSEAD academics, Chan Kim and Renee Mauborgne, argue that competing head-on in today's overcrowded industries results in nothing but a 'bloody red ocean of rivals fighting over a shrinking profit pool'. Based on a study of 150 strategic moves over a 100-year period, they argue that tomorrow's winners will succeed not by battling in red oceans but by creating 'blue oceans of uncontested market space ripe for growth'.

In a red ocean you fight competitors with tooth and nail in an existing market space. In a blue ocean you swim jauntily in an uncontested market space – new demand is created and competitors become irrelevant.

Such strategic moves create genuine 'value innovation', or 'powerful leaps in value for both firm and buyers, rendering rivals obsolete'.

They quote examples such as Apple's iTunes and Cirque du Soleil. Apple created a new market space by teaming up with the music companies to offer legal online music downloading, thereby consigning pioneer Napster (the bane of the music companies) to history. Cirque du Soleil reinvented the circus industry by blending it with ballet to create a new market space.

They further argue that the conventional choice of generic strategy between differentiation and low cost is also sub-optimal. That is the traditional choice faced by competitors in a 'red ocean'. 'Blue ocean' strategy enables the firm to do both, offering a differentiated product to a new market space at a cost sufficiently low to deter further entrants.

The holy grail of 'blue ocean' strategy is to create: Differentiated Product + Low Cost = Value Innovation.

They put forward six principles for creating and capturing 'blue oceans':

- Reconstruct market boundaries
- Focus on the big picture
- Reach beyond existing demand
- Get the strategic sequence right
- Overcome organisational hurdles
- Build execution into strategy.

Kim and Mauborgne challenge you to fundamentally rethink the rules of the game in your industry. The key success factors you drew up in Chapter 4 and revisited in your brainstorming sessions in Chapter 6 may need to be radically rethought, perhaps even, and this is their first port of call, eliminated:

- Which KSFs that the industry takes for granted should be *eliminated*?
- Which KSFs should be *reduced well below* the industry's standard?
- Which KSFs should be *raised well above* the industry's standard?
- Which KSFs should be *created* that the industry has never offered?

In short, how can these KSFs be revised so that a new value curve is created, one which breaks the trade-off between differentiation and low-cost strategies?

The model is highly stimulating but has to be applied with care, especially for small and medium-sized enterprises. Nine times out of ten, strategy development will be about improving strategic position in 'red ocean' markets. 'Blue ocean' markets may exist, but they are riskier – often greatly riskier. For every Apple iTunes and Cirque du Soleil, there are scores of attempted 'blue ocean' strategies that have foundered.

As Igor Ansoff highlighted in Chapter 5, new products to new markets carry a degree of risk orders of magnitude higher than new products to existing markets or existing products to new markets. iTunes was a new product to the new market, for Apple, of online downloading. It worked. Many such don't.

Risk, however, is no argument for debunking Kim and Mauborgne. It is an argument for embracing their 'blue ocean' thinking here and subjecting it to the rigours of risk analysis and sensitivity testing in Chapter 9 of this book.

Making the strategic investment decision

You have drawn up two or three strategic alternatives aimed at bridging the strategic gap in your business. They were mutually exclusive, so you can take only one of them. How do you evaluate them and select the best?

The answer is straightforward in theory. Assuming your main goal is to maximise shareholder value, and subject to goals relating to other stakeholder interests (see Chapter 2), you should choose the alternative that gives you the highest return for the lowest risk.

How you get there is not so straightforward. There is a spectrum of methods, ranging from the dangerously complex (real option valuation) to the dangerously simple (impact on earnings).

The best method is discounted cash flow ('DCF') analysis, but it is tricky and hard to get right, even by business school graduates. Here is not the place to describe how to apply it. This is not a book on finance.

Instead we shall look at a rather simple method, the payback method. It has its faults, many of them, but its virtue is its simplicity. As long as you are aware of its faults and use it with care, this method should for the most part do the job.

But before starting, there are three fundamentals in making the strategic investment decision that need to be borne in mind whatever the method chosen.

The first is the nature of making an investment. It usually means a cash outlay today that should give you cash, or other benefits, flowing in for years to come. Investment tends to be a one-time, upfront cost, leading to recurring annual benefits.

Second is 'sunken costs'. When you're comparing the viability of strategic alternatives, any cash you've already spent has to be forgotten about. You must take into account only what *extra* cash you need to spend on an alternative from this day forward to generate the benefits expected.

Finally, cash today and cash tomorrow are different things. Cash invested today in a strategic alternative has a higher value than cash generated in future years, not just because of inflation but because of the 'opportunity cost of capital' – cash today could have been invested elsewhere to generate a real return until tomorrow.

This is how to apply the payback method for evaluating investment proposals.

Work out the cost of the investment, say £I. Assess the annual benefits from the investment, namely the difference between the extra cash inflow (from revenues) and the extra cash outflow (from expenses) generated each year as a result of the investment. If the annual benefits are different each year, take their average over the first five years, £B/year. Divide B into I, and this gives you the 'payback', the number of years taken for the cash costs of the investment to be recouped.

If payback is *four years* or less, that could well be a sound investment. (This is equivalent to a 9% annual rate of return over a five-year period, assuming – conservatively – no benefits beyond five years, due to obsolescence, competitive response, etc.) But don't jump on it. Work out the payback on the other strategic alternatives as well. They may have an even lower payback.

If you believe your investment is going to give you a longer-term advantage and could last all of 10 years, then an investment with a longer payback may still be beneficial. You might give serious consideration to an investment with a payback of six to seven years. It'll be riskier, of course, because all sorts of things could happen to your competitive position over time.

Next, work out the 'net benefits' of the strategic alternative, the total benefits over the five years less the investment cost. If the alternative has a longer-term horizon, with benefits taking a few years to kick in and blossoming only after five, six or seven years, you should opt for DCF analysis.

There are, however, other elements. The above has focused on one side of the story, the financial. What are the benefits of pursuing an alternative in terms of meeting your firm's non-financial goals? These may need to be factored into the evaluation.

Then there is risk. Each alternative will be more or less risky than the other. The alternative that promises the highest returns for the lowest investment outlay may be unacceptably risky. Another alternative that offers modest payback for a modest outlay may be virtually risk-free. How risky are your proposed alternatives?

It may be helpful for you to lay out the strategic alternatives in a table, along with their investment cost, annual benefits, payback, net benefits, non-financial benefits and risk, as shown in Table 7.2.

The table will guide you on which of the three alternatives is the most financially beneficial. It should be the one with the highest net benefits and with an acceptable payback – subject to the three fundamental provisos above concerning the time value of money.

Table 7.2 **The payback approach to evaluating strategic alternatives**

	Unit	Strategic alternatives		
		A	B	C
Financial benefits				
Investment costs = I	£			
Average annual cash benefits over 5 years = B	£/Year			
Payback = I / B	Years			
Total cash benefits over 5 years = TB = B × 5	£			
Net benefits = TB – I	£			
Risk	L/M/H			
Non-financial benefits		•	•	• ....
		•	•	• ....
Non-financial dis-benefits		•	•	• ....
		•	•	• ....

Note that the alternative with the fastest payback is not necessarily the best – net benefits may be too small, even though they are the most rapidly achieved. But if the alternative with the fastest payback is not mutually exclusive with the one that has the highest net benefits, perhaps you could do both?

The most financially beneficial alternative from the table, however, may be the riskiest. In this case you may choose to opt for an alternative with a lower return but commensurately lower risk.

Once you have concluded which is the best alternative to pursue, think about how it can be enhanced. Perhaps one or two promising profit growth options from another alternative can be added – or swapped with a less promising option from the winning alternative. What impact would that have on the evaluation? Would it ease the strategic investment decision?

That is the payback method. Use it, but be wary. It is effectively a short-cut, a simple approach. Or should that read simplistic?

It has serious drawbacks. It doesn't take into account the time value of money, nor the possible lumpiness or risk of annual cash flows. And it ignores cash flows beyond the payback period, thereby favouring investments with short-term returns.

If your strategic investment decision is complex, and especially if benefits are late developing, do it properly through DCF analysis. If you don't feel comfortable with that, engage a specialist.

Finally, whichever approach you use, the most financially beneficial alternative may not be the most beneficial to your firm overall. It may have the most negative implications for your non-financial goals.

The strategic investment decision is seldom clear-cut. The financials are often hard to evaluate and even then there may be a trade-off between financial return, risk and meeting non-financial goals.

The decision is yours.

Essential tip

The financial consequences of making the wrong strategic investment decision may be severe. If you are in doubt, get some help with the financial analysis. A few thousand pounds for advice up front might save you tens or even hundreds of thousands of pounds down the line.

Essential example

Sainsbury's fights back

Our family moved from one village to another in south-west London in the late 1990s. As one of the plus points of the move, I announced to my wife that not only was there a Sainsbury's supermarket within walking distance of our house-to-be but a Sainsbury's hypermarket too at the other end of the village. That this news was greeted not with a cheer but a groan came as a surprise. Sainsbury's was surely a byword in quality grocery shopping? Was it not the case that 'good food costs less at Sainsbury's'? My wife knew better. What had gone wrong?

Sainsbury's at the time still had around 20% share of the UK grocery market, though it had recently been overtaken by Tesco. Asda was some way behind on 13%, with Safeway (later absorbed by Morrison's), Waitrose and Marks & Spencer in single figures. But what did Sainsbury's stand for? It had long ceded top-quality products to Waitrose and M&S. Asda and Safeway were pitched as low-cost. And Tesco had managed to improve quality, a far cry from its cheap and cheerful image of the 1970s, while still retaining competitive pricing.

My wife, and presumably many other shoppers, saw Sainsbury's as offering medium-quality product at medium to high prices.

Being stuck in the middle is never a good place to be strategically. But Sainsbury's position was worse. What really maddened my wife was returning home with only three-quarters of her shopping done. Extraordinarily for such a prominent, nationwide retailer, all too often the shelves were empty. Or the fruit and vegetables were soggy.

And even customer service, the pride and joy of the traditional grocer, J. Sainsbury, in the days before self-service, was miserable. It reeked of an organisation that had lost its way in its core business, with management seemingly more excited by opportunities in town centre mini-markets (Sainsbury's Local, to rival Tesco Metro), DIY sheds (Homebase), banking and overseas (Egypt, USA).

New management in 2000 undertook a business transformation programme and attacked the issue of availability of stock, investing a hefty £3 billion in distribution, including four state-of-the-art automated regional distribution centres. But the unproven automation system turned out to be flawed and availability worsened.

Justin King took over what he later described as a 'burning platform' in early 2004. He immediately carried out a mass consultation with customers (one million letters sent out, attracting a quarter of a million replies, one of which was mine), asking them what they really wanted from Sainsbury's. Unsurprisingly, they wanted the company to get back to basics – food on the shelves, of good quality, with helpful service and competitive pricing.

King saw a huge strategic gap between Sainsbury's, now down to 15% market share (below Asda), and Tesco, up to 28% – in virtually every key success factor. In cost (economies of scale were now with Tesco), quality, availability, premises and service, Sainsbury's was woefully short of the 'ideal player of tomorrow'.

King's response was the launch of the 'Making Sainsbury's great again' strategy, where the wholesale refocus of the group on the core grocery business was pledged, along with:

■ pricing to be matched with Tesco;

■ corporate HQ cost savings of £400m, with the proceeds to finance price cutting;

■ refurbishment of a quarter of the (under-invested) estate;

■ 3000 new jobs on the shop floor to improve the customer experience;

■ reactivation of former depots, bypassing the newly automated ones, ensuring competitive availability even at a hike in cost.

His strategy was well received in the City. Sales dipped and profits tumbled in 2005 and 2006, but the strategic focus held firm. Sainsbury's started to improve steadily in quality, availability, premises, service and price – and customer perception. The strategic gap has largely been bridged.

Proof of that is in the numbers. Like-for-like sales grew in 32 consecutive quarters to the end of 2012 – despite the pushes of Waitrose, Aldi, Lidl, Iceland, online sales and convenience stores, let alone of the other Big 4 chains. Market share has been gained every year and now stands at close to 17%, with Tesco slipping back from 32% to around 30%.

> Yet concerns remain. Some analysts observe that customers seem to have benefited more from King's strategy than shareholders. Sainsbury's revenues are forecast at £23 billion in 2013, with pre-tax profit of £750m. Morrison's is forecast to turn over £5 billion less, but with £140m more profit.
>
> Sainsbury's still has work to do ...

Bridging the gap for a start-up

In Chapter 6 we targeted the gap between your competitive position upon launch and that of where you need to be three years hence – by which time your distinct competitive advantage must have become or is due to become sustainable.

But how to get there?

There is nothing special here about a start-up. In bridging the strategic gap, the process is the same as for an established business:

- *Confirm your generic strategy* – low cost or differentiated. Don't opt for a focused strategy, or you run the risk of being stuck in the middle – medium cost, medium differentiation, a recipe for business failure. A focused strategy is a luxury afforded to a more mature company with economies of scale; for a start-up, be either low-cost or differentiated and do not waiver.

- *Shaping profit growth options* – crafting a set of initiatives to bridge the gap in the segments to be invested in, including those needed to protect yourself against competitive response (see possible solutions in Chapter 6). For a start-up, of course, all segments are new and to be invested in – by definition, there are as yet no segments for holding or exit; group them into two or three strategic alternatives.

- *Evaluate the alternatives* – using the payback method as above or, if you feel comfortable with it, DCF analysis.

- *Refine as necessary* the best alternative and make your strategic investment decision.

To reiterate, to survive your launch you must have a distinct competitive advantage – with a low-cost or differentiated strategy. To survive three to five years out, that competitive advantage must be sustainable.

Having identified that strategic gap in Chapter 6, your strategy development process of Chapter 7 must bridge that gap and deliver your firm a sustainable competitive advantage by Year 5.

Business strategic risks and opportunities

At the end of Chapter 3, you pieced together all the key risks and opportunities associated with future market demand. You did the same for those concerning industry competition at the end of Chapter 4. Now you should do the same for those relating to your chosen business strategy.

You have already done much of the work. In evaluating your strategic alternatives, one of the main considerations, factored directly into the evaluation, was risk.

Furthermore, the evaluation worked out the impact of each strategic alternative on your business – in terms of net benefits, both financial and non-financial.

All you need do now is disaggregate, roughly, the main risk components of each alternative (remember that each alternative is an aggregated grouping of a whole range of profit growth options) and assess them – by likelihood of occurrence and by impact should they occur.

Remember we are only interested in what we defined in Chapter 3 as 'big' risks, those which are at least reasonably likely to occur and with reasonable impact upon occurrence.

These 'big' business strategic risks and opportunities will be blended with those of market demand, competition and corporate strategy in Chapter 9 and assessed for balance and viability.

Essential case study

Extramural Ltd Strategic Review, 2013

Chapter 7: Business strategy

Richard and Jane Davies have sketched out their vision of the ideal player in the school activity tour business in a brainstorming session on the River Dart – see Chapter 6. Their challenge now is how to get from Extramural's competitive position today to as close as achievable to the ideal player in three to five years' time. How do they bridge the gap?

▶

First things first: they need to firm up on Extramural's generic strategy. Brutally, it could be argued that Extramural is but a me-too player to market leader ActivTours – hence the large differential in market share, competitive position and operating margin.

That would be an unflattering assessment, one that underappreciates Extramural's presence and position in the market. And yet it has elements of truth. The company doesn't really stand out in the market.

The Davieses look at the generic options. Extramural is not a low-cost player – there are a couple of these and one is doing quite well – and has no intention of becoming one. Extramural is a reasonably differentiated player, offering a higher-quality product than many on the market, though no higher than ActivTours or STL, and focusing a bit more on combined learning/activity tours than its competitors.

The answer is clear. Extramural needs to aim for a fuller differentiation. It needs to be perceived in the minds of teachers, beyond debate, as the pre-eminent provider of learning-cum-activity tours. For any such tour, Extramural must be first port of call. This would have a number of benefits, including:

- A clear differentiation from ActivTours, even though the latter offers virtually the same combined tours (these two and STL ape each other mercilessly), for marketing purposes.
- Greater resilience in times of market downturn, for instance in the Nightmare! scenario (see Chapter 6).
- The opportunity further down the road to offer such differentiated tours at a slight price premium.
- The differentiation should serve to raise customer perceptions of Extramural's pure activity tours, perhaps thinking that the educational ethos of the company will infuse otherwise non-educational activities.

The Davieses might even go one step further. They could opt for a focus strategy and concentrate the whole company on school activity tours, selling off one or both of their other businesses, educational tours and day camps, to invest further in school activity tours. Such a focus strategy could also serve to lower unit costs over time through the experience curve and economies of scale, narrowing the cost differential from ActivTours. But that is corporate strategy, for discussion in the next chapter.

Next, the Davieses consider how the business should be repositioned. They revisit the strategic position chart they drew up in Chapter 6 and set their sights on these targets (see Figure 7.2):

■ Strengthen competitive position in pure activity tours through addressing shortcomings identified in the customer survey.

■ Boost competitive position in combined learning/activity tours through a strategy of differentiation – using the forthcoming budgeted campaign to roll out the language/activity product as a springboard for repositioning.

■ Withdraw from football/activity tours, which make little contribution once marketing costs are fully attributed.

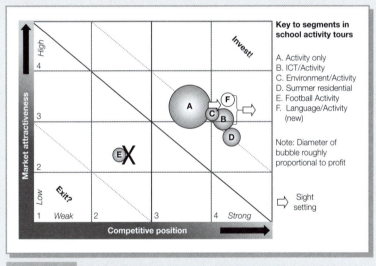

Figure 7.2   **Extramural Ltd: target strategic position in school activity tours**

The Davieses then proceed to develop more specific profit growth initiatives. The immediate priority has to be improved customer service – indeed a total, radical overhaul of customer service. Sasha's customer survey revealed that teachers unambiguously rated ActivTours' service as superior to Extramural's, all the way through the process – from helping with admin pre-arrival, to care and attention on site, accommodation and perks to teachers during the stay and post-visit tidying up.

Sasha also did some useful competitor research and, using a clever variety of sources, including ex-employees of competitors, dug up some illuminating findings. The Davieses had always been proud of their customer retention rate, typically convincing 60–70% of teachers to rebook their school trips for the following year before leaving their current tour. They were shocked to learn that ActivTours averaged a customer rebooking rate of 83%, while one competitor with just the one centre managed over 90%!

The Davieses suspected that their whole marketing approach might be flawed. Coming from the package tour industry, their philosophy had always been marketing driven – heavy marketing, pack in the punters, deliver as promised, more heavy marketing. It seemed that ActivTours used an entirely different approach: modest marketing, super-please the punters, make sure they come back, and rely on them to market to others by word of mouth.

Not only did ActivTours's approach seem to boost customer retention rates, but also profits – their total marketing spend was well below that of Extramural, despite their being a 50% larger operation.

The Davieses held a workshop with selected site managers and their heads of sales and marketing to tackle this issue head-on. They drew up a multi-pronged campaign to raise customer service, highlights of which were:

- A complete redrawing of the in-house staff training programme, promoting through every stage the concept of 'super-pleasing' the customer
- The introduction of a customer loyalty programme, including perks and gifts given to teachers for rebooking pre-departure and again upon arrival the following year
- The introduction of a customer guarantee programme, including no-questions-asked rebates for any activities laid on which failed to match customer expectations
- From immediate effect, the introduction of an 'Instructor of the Week' award at every centre, voted for by both teachers and children.

This 'super-pleasing challenge' was by no means the only profit growth initiative the Davieses derived from their strategic review. Other highlights included (see Table 7.3):

■ Acquire one new centre per year over the next three years, filling in regional gaps, especially in the North-East, and perhaps one more in France – finance for which could possibly be provided by sale of a business (see the next chapter on corporate strategy).

■ Roll out the new ICT suites across all centres, building on the popularity of the suites already introduced at two centres, while offering modest discounts for ICT/activity tours at centres not yet re-equipped.

■ Roll out the language lab trialled at the Exeter centre to another five centres (thereby, along with the ICT suites, reaffirming Extramural's differentiation strategy).

Table 7.3 | **Extramural Ltd: profit growth initiatives to bridge the gap in school activity tours**

Strategic repositioning alternative	Segment	Profit growth initiatives	
		Short-term	Long-term
Invest	Activity only	• Instructor of the week rating	• Staff training in service • Customer loyalty scheme • Customer guarantee scheme • Regional site roll out
	ICT	• Discount for aged suite sites	• Roll out new suites
Hold	Environment	• None	• Research new themes
	Summer	• Offer educational clubs	• Demand-based pricing
New	Language	• Link more to curriculum	• Roll out language labs
Exit	Football	• Talk to Footie4Kids	
Business as a whole		• Tweak advertising message	• Improve career progression • Restructure sales • Focus marketing spend

- More demand-based pricing for the summer residential camps, with bigger discounts for early booking and premiums where achievable for last-minute booking.
- Withdraw from football/activity tours, perhaps negotiating a reciprocal referral scheme with Footie4Kids.
- For the business as a whole, tweak the advertising message to pitch Extramural as a provider of learning-cum-activity tours, as distinct from an activity tour provider which also offers educational activities.
- Focus the marketing message as such, invest in a marketing push in 2013, highlighting Extramural's state-of-the-art ICT suites and language labs, then reduce spend from 2013's projected 12% of revenue to ActivTours's 7% by 2015 – relying on improved customer retention rates to maintain occupancy levels.

The result of the strategic repositioning and profit growth initiatives should be a significant strengthening over time of Extramural's competitive position in the school activity tours business. Richard inserts a new column into the table of Chapter 5 and adjusts Extramural's rating to reflect the impact of the new business strategy. Re-ratings can be justified as follows (see Table 7.4):

- With a planned 30% increase in bed capacity, Extramural's market share rating rises to around 4, up from 3.4.
- This should bring some scale economies in areas such as purchasing and marketing, raising the cost competitiveness rating from 3.5 to 3.75.
- With investment rolled out in ICT suites and language labs, along with regular updating of activity facilities, the rating against product quality and range should rise from 4 to 4.25.
- The 'super-pleasing challenge' should improve the customer service rating from an unacceptable 3 to a target in excess of 4.

These strategic improvements against key success factors could boost Extramural's competitive position in school activity tours from 3.8 to 4.2. The gap with ActivTours should be narrowed.

But the analysis to date has assumed that ActivTours will sit still and allow Extramural to narrow the gap. This is unlikely. Richard and Jane think about what they would do if they were running

| Table 7.4 | Extramural Ltd: future competitive position in school activity tours | | | | |

Key success factors: school activity tours	Weighting	ActivTours today	Extramural today	Extramural in three years	ActivTours response?
Market share	20%	5	3.4	**4**	5
Cost factors: Economies of scale, occupancy	25%	4	3.5	**3.75**	4
Management factors: Sales, marketing, CRM	10%	4	5	5	4
Differentiation factors: Safety and security	10%	5	4.5	4.5	5
Product quality and range	20%	4.5	4	**4.25**	**4.75**
Customer service and delivery	15%	4.5	3	**4.25**	**4.75**
Competitive Position	**100%**	**4.5**	**3.8**	**4.2**	**4.6**

Key: 1 = Weak, 2 = Tenable, 3 = Favourable, 4 = Strong, 5 = Dominant

ActivTours, faced with a resurgent Extramural. They may well acquire a new site or two, probably on the Continent, given that their regional coverage in the UK is all but complete. They could invest in new ICT suites or language labs themselves. But do they need to? That is not how they position themselves. They will for sure poach any new successful ideas Extramural introduces in customer service, such as the customer guarantee scheme. They could raise their competitive position to a rating of 4.6 – see the final column of Table 7.2.

But there is little ActivTours can do to stop Extramural repositioning as a learning-cum-activity tour provider and transforming its customer service levels. ActivTours could raise the bar yet further, but Extramural could follow.

The Davieses' strategy seems set to narrow the gap. A gap may well remain, but it will be no chasm.

Finally, Richard Davies is not one to embark on a series of profit growth initiatives without testing the financial implications. Richard is a numbers man, Jane being more into concepts. Some of the initiatives are no-brainers, with readily identifiable and likely rapid paybacks – such as the range of customer service initiatives planned.

Others, like rolling out ICT suites and language labs, let alone the addition of one new centre a year, require more detailed financial planning. So Richard arms himself with the *FT Essential Guide to Business Planning* and draws up some Profit & Loss forecasts for his school activity tour business (excluding the two other businesses of educational tours and day camps).

These are his findings:

- School activity tour revenues are forecast to rise from £13.3m to £18.9m, up from the pre-strategic review forecast of £17.9m due to one additional centre and slightly improved average revenue per child, offset by a temporary drop in average occupancy from 48% to 46%.

- Gross profit less marketing expense, or 'contribution to non-marketing overheads', is forecast to grow from £6.6m in 2012 to £10.4m by 2015, an average growth rate of 16% per year – exceeding the pre-strategic review forecast of £8.7m by around 20%.

- Each new centre has a forecast payback of 4.8 years.

- The ICT suite and language lab investments have forecast paybacks of 2.6 and 3.7 years.

- The business is poised in 2015 to achieve further growth in contribution of 11% per year to 2017, assuming no further site acquisitions, as occupancy rates firm through site maturity and higher customer retention rates, and prices are nudged up to reflect the quality of the ICT, language and other educational facilities provided at Extramural centres.

The Davieses are delighted with their new strategy for their school activity tours business and present it at an offsite meeting at an Exmoor inn on to their senior and middle managers. It goes down a treat and all head for the oak-beamed, stag-themed bar feeling remotivated and inspired to take the business to the next level.

The Davieses do likewise for their two other businesses, the outcome of which we shall review in the next chapter on corporate strategy.

Essential checklist on bridging the business strategy gap

■ Draw up a business strategy to bridge the strategic gap in your business. If yours is a multi-business company, do the same for each of your businesses.

■ Opt for one, but only one, of the three generic strategies:

— *Low-cost* – offering a product (or service) to the market on a par with those of your competitors but at a lower cost

— *Differentiation* – offering a product to the market that is distinctive in one or more key success factors, such as product quality, distribution or customer service, and potentially enabling a price premium

— *Focus* – tailoring your offering to a niche segment and enabling you to offer a differentiated product at a cost driven lower through economies of scale and the experience curve effect.

■ Reposition your business strategically by investing in certain product/market segments, holding in others, entering new ones and exiting those in unattractive markets where your competitive position is weak.

■ Consider a range of profit growth options for each of your segments and group them together into strategic alternatives.

■ Evaluate which of these strategic alternatives to pursue, using the simple (but simplistic) payback method or, preferably, the more complex discounted cash flow analysis.

■ Assess the big risks and opportunities of making this strategic investment decision.

8

Bridging the gap: corporate strategy

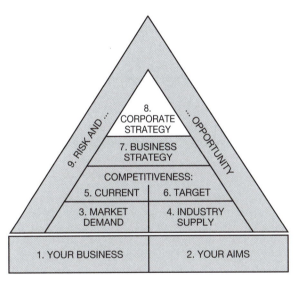

66 Put all your eggs in one basket and then watch that basket.

Mark Twain

In this chapter

- Optimising the corporate portfolio
  - Essential tool: The growth/share matrix
- Creating value through mergers, acquisitions and alliances
  - Essential tool: Parenting value

- Building strategically valuable resources
  - Essential tool: Building core competences
- Corporate strategic risks and opportunities

Is yours a multi-business firm?

If so, this chapter applies to you. In Chapter 7, you sought to bridge the strategic gap through improving competitiveness in each of your businesses. That was business strategy. Now for corporate strategy.

There are two schools of thought in corporate strategy:

- The market positioning school – where strategy should be focused at the level of the business, where all meaningful competition resides, and corporate strategy is limited to portfolio planning
- The resource-based school – where strategy should be focused on leveraging the resources and capabilities (or 'competences') of the corporation as a whole.

Both schools have their merits and this chapter sets out how to extract the best from each school.

Optimising the corporate portfolio

In the early 1980s, the new CEO of General Electric, Jack Welch, asked management guru Peter Drucker for advice. He responded with two questions that arguably changed the course of Welch's tenure: 'If you weren't already in a business, would you enter it today? And if the answer is no, what are you going to do about it?'.

This led directly to Welch's corporate strategy that every one of GE's businesses had to be either number 1 or number 2 in its sphere. If not, it would be fixed, sold or shut. The strategy was brutal, but effective.

Corporate strategy is not necessarily that different from business strategy. Often it can be just a timing or definitional issue – a business unit of today may be a stand-alone corporation when sold to management tomorrow.

Nevertheless, corporate strategy tools are designed to address different questions. Whereas business strategy sets out to ask how a business can obtain a sustainable competitive advantage, corporate strategy asks three questions:

- Which businesses should you be investing (your scarce resources) in?

■ Which businesses should you be acquiring or divesting?

■ Which resources common to all businesses should you focus on?

The second question will be looked at in the next section on adding value in mergers, acquisitions and alliances. The third on the resource-based view of strategy will follow. Here the focus is on which businesses you should invest in.

You have already met the main tool to do just that, the attractiveness/advantage matrix. In Chapter 6, you used it to determine the optimal balance of product/market segments within a business. Now you can use it to determine the optimal balance of businesses within a corporation.

And there is another terrific tool which you can use, similar but with a different nuance – The Boston Consulting Group growth share matrix (see the essential tool text box).

These matrices should give you a clear picture on:

■ Which businesses you should invest in

■ Which businesses you should hold and improve performance in

■ Which businesses you should exit

■ Which new businesses you should enter.

You should use them as set out in Chapter 6, substituting the word 'business' for 'segment' all the way through.

Again, the value of these matrices is only as good as the data and analysis put in. Your assessment of market attractiveness and competitive position for each business in the attractiveness/advantage matrix must be rigorous and dispassionate.

Essential tool

The growth/share matrix

The Boston Consulting Group's growth share matrix, along with its catchy menagerie of cows and dogs, is one of those strategy tools which has stood the test of time. It first appeared in the late 1960s and is as widely used today as ever.

Its aims are essentially the same as those of the attractiveness/advantage matrix, charting the relative position of the businesses analysed for the purposes of resource allocation.

▶

Where it differs is in its choice of parameters:

- Instead of a somewhat subjective assessment of *market attractiveness*, it opts for one measurable parameter, *market demand growth*.
- Instead of a somewhat subjective assessment of *competitive position*, it opts for one measurable parameter, *relative market share*.

The growth share matrix offers, in essence, an objective, measurable proxy for the attractiveness/advantage matrix.

Here is how to use it. Draw up a 2 × 2 matrix with these axes:

- Relative market share ('RMS') along the x-axis – not market share in itself, but your market share relative to that of your *leading* competitor. Market share on its own is no indicator of relative strength; having a market share of 20% may be a strength in a highly fragmented market where your nearest competitor has 10% and most other main competitors are in single figures, but that 20% takes on a different complexion if you are in a concentrated market where the leader has 40%. In the first market, your relative market share would be 2.0*x*, but in the second it would be 0.5*x* – implying very different prospects for sustaining competitive advantage.
- Market growth along the y-axis, taken as the forecast annual average growth rate in real terms over the next three to five years (as derived in Chapter 3).

Plot your product/market segments accordingly and reveal the following:

- The 'stars': those segments that are in the top right quadrant, where you have high share in a fast-growing market
- The 'cash cows': those in the bottom right segment, where you have high share in a slow-growing market
- The 'question marks': those in the top left quadrant, where you have low share in a fast-growing market
- The 'dogs': those in the bottom left quadrant, where you have low share in a slow-growing market.

Other things being equal, you should invest in your stars, harvest your cash cows, divest your dogs and analyse carefully the risks and returns of investing in your question marks.

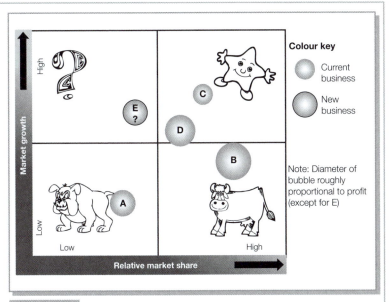

Figure 8.1 **The growth share matrix: an example**

Source: Adapted from the BCG Portfolio Matrix from the Product Portfolio Matrix ©
1970, The Boston Consulting Group

Take an example – see Figure 8.1. Here you may consider the
following strategic options worthy of further analysis:

■ Milking of cash cow B

■ Holding and possible investment in borderline cash cow/star D

■ Investment in definitive star C

■ Likely entry to borderline question mark/star E

■ Harvesting or exit from dog A.

How is the portfolio of segments in your business? Hopefully your
main segments, from which you derive most revenues, should
find themselves positioned in the right-hand quadrants, the cash
cows and stars. Any dogs? Should you sell or close them? Any
question marks? How can you make them stellar?

Essential tip

Whether your preference is to use the attractiveness/advantage matrix or the growth share matrix, or both, in corporate portfolio analysis is up to you. But be aware of the limitations of each.

The former is criticised for being too subjective, the latter for being potentially misleading, market growth not necessarily being a proxy for market attractiveness (growth may be fast, but there may be a glut of competitors) and relative market share not necessarily being a proxy for competitive position (the market leader may be on the way down – think of fallen giants such as IBM in personal computers).

My advice is to use both matrices, observe any differences in the resultant conclusions and examine what lies beneath them.

Creating value through mergers, acquisitions and alliances

Mergers, acquisitions and alliances (together, 'M&A') have been with us since the dawn of capitalism. But more often than not they fail to create value.

The reason is simple: acquirers pay too much to gain control.

And the reasons behind that are also clear:

- Managers are often hell-bent on closing the deal – they have made up their minds that this is what they want to do, for whatever reason, genuinely strategic or personal empire building, and they will not allow prolonged negotiations and an ever-rising price tag to prevent them from getting the deal done.
- Managers do insufficient strategic analysis pre-deal along the lines set out in this tool.
- Managers pay inadequate attention to due diligence.
- Managers underestimate the difficulties of post-deal integration and the inevitable delay in achieving aspired merger benefits.

The theory behind M&A value creation is simple. We start with the premise that acquisition of company B by A will be of strategic benefit to A. Then:

- The acquisition will create synergies, i.e. benefits in cost saving or revenue enhancement that will be tapped by the joining forces of A and B.

▧ The value of the AB will exceed the stand-alone values of A and B by the value of the synergies.

▧ Company A will be unable to buy B at its stand-alone value – shareholders of B will demand a premium to the pre-bid price to cede control.

▧ The acquisition will be successful, as defined by creating, not destroying, value for the shareholders of A, if the synergy value is greater than the premium paid by A for B.

The challenge in M&A, therefore, is to work out the synergy value.

There are seven main tasks in the M&A assessment process:

▧ Confirm strategic rationale:
  – What are your strategic objectives?
  – Is acquisition the appropriate route?
  – What are your transferable strengths?

▧ Select the right target:
  – Set criteria for strategic fit – both screening ('must-have') and ranking ('should-have') criteria
  – Prioritise the criteria
  – Screen the candidates rigorously – root out those that fail to pass through the sieve
  – Rank the candidates.

▧ Assess the risks:
  – Do the 'due diligence' analysis – financial, legal, environmental and especially (though I would say this!) strategic
  – Use the 'Suns & Clouds Chart' (see Chapter 9) to assess the balance of risk and opportunity.

▧ Value the stand-alone entities:
  – Value the target, preferably using discounted cash flow (DCF) analysis, or other methods such as comparable trading multiples (e.g. price/earnings ratio or P/E) or comparable transaction multiples (e.g. enterprise value to sales, or to earnings before interest, tax, depreciation and amortisation – EBITDA) for companies operating in the same or similar industry sectors to you
  – Value your own company on the same basis.

▧ Identify the potential synergies:
  – Revenue enhancement opportunities – cross-selling and/or combined selling opportunities, net of custom likely to be lost as a result of the merger

- Operating cost savings – through, for example, combined purchasing power, economies of scale or rationalisation of overhead
- Capital cost savings – investment that can be avoided through the merging of plant, equipment, IT and the like.

▓ Value the net synergies:
- Value the synergy opportunities identified, slot them into your DCF or profit & loss model and observe the impact
- Apply the red pen – allow for over-optimism by slashing revenue enhancement synergy value by 50% and cost saving synergies, which are more under your control, by 20–25%
- Deduct the direct costs of merger – allow for transaction costs pre-deal plus the costs of integrating the two companies post-deal, typically grossly underestimated in both extent and duration.

▓ Ensure added value:
- Assess the acquisition premium – that needed to acquire control of the target is typically of the order of 30–40%
- If your synergy value is below the acquisition premium, walk away
- If it is above, return to the Suns & Clouds Chart (see Chapter 9); if any risk seems of sufficient likelihood to make such a dent in synergy value that the latter falls below the acquisition premium, you may need to walk away
- If it is above, and you are happy with the balance of risk and opportunity, close the deal.

Again, remember: more than half of all acquisitions destroy value. This is because the acquirer overpaid. You don't want to be part of that statistic.

Essential tip

Take great care in any merger, acquisition or alliance. Most fail!

Remember one of the eight principles preached by Tom Peters and Robert Waterman in *In Search of Excellence*, published in 1982: stick to the knitting.

Focus on what you know and do best.

This advice was reinforced by Chris Zook in his *Profit from the Core*. Successful companies operate in an F-E-R cycle:

■ Focus on, understand and reach full potential in the core business

■ Expand into logical adjacent businesses surrounding that core

■ Redefine pre-emptively the core business in response to market turbulence.

In other words, beware diversification, whether organically or through M&A.

Essential tool

Parenting value

Not only do most mergers and acquisitions fail to create value, but so too do most head offices! This was the path-breaking finding of Michael Goold, Andrew Campbell and Marcus Alexander in their 1994 book, *Corporate-Level Strategy: Creating Value in Multi-Business Companies*. They found that the head office, or the corporate centre, more often than not failed to create value in a multi-business company. It destroyed value.

Goold, Campbell and Alexander encourage the strategist to think of the corporate centre as the intermediary between the investor and the business unit. The centre can add value to the business unit if there are net synergies between them, offsetting dissynergies such as:

■ Wrong decision-making by the centre due to distance from the front line and often unfamiliarity with the business unit's market environment and key success factors

■ The demotivating aspect of distancing front-line managers from their investors

■ The overhead expense of HQ, often high

■ The acquisition premium, where the business was bought rather than organically built, and which is frequently way too high (see above).

They believe that multi-business companies can create

synergistic value by developing the right 'parenting skills', exploiting the right 'parenting opportunities' and establishing a 'parenting advantage' by owning the business.

In essence the centre, or 'parent', should view its business units using the same lens as the acquirer – to create value, there should be synergies not just between businesses but between centre and business unit. That will create a parenting advantage.

They go further. If a parent's ownership of a business creates an advantage but a competing parent would create a bigger advantage, the parent should consider selling the business at a healthy sale premium and invest the proceeds in a business where its own parenting advantage is maximised.

This is a highly instructive insight no matter the size of the firm. If another firm can run one of your businesses better than you can, think about selling it for a healthy sum and use the cash to build up another business which you can run better than others can.

Building strategically valuable resources

If strategic thinking was dominated in the 1970s by BCG's Experience Curve (see Chapter 7) and growth share matrix (this chapter) and in the 1980s by Michael Porter's five forces (Chapter 4), the 1990s can be viewed in retrospect as the time of the resource-based school of corporate strategy.

In essence, this states that a company's strategy should be focused on leveraging the resources and capabilities of the company as a whole.

Chief trumpeters of this school were Gary Hamel and C. K. Prahalad – see the adjacent text box – but other business academics made contributions that were arguably as important. One such was Rob Grant and his Resources and Capabilities Strengths/Importance matrix. Perhaps the final word, however, came from Collis and Montgomery's work on strategically valuable resources in 1995, which neatly blends the resource-based view with the market-based views of Porter, BCG et al.

For a resource to be strategically valuable, they stated, it must pass five external market tests of its value:

■ The test of inimitability: is it hard to copy? They identify four main barriers to imitation (physical uniqueness, path dependency, causal ambiguity and economic deterrence).

■ The test of durability: how long will it last? They give the example of the evergreen Disney brand, which has outlasted the death of Walt by decades.

■ The test of appropriability: who captures the value that the resource creates? They give the example of leveraged buyout firms, where the key resource of contact lists often walks out of the door as executives quit to start up their own funds.

■ The test of substitutability: can a unique resource be trumped by a different resource?

■ The test of competitive superiority: whose resource is really better?

Use these guidelines to identify which of your resources are strategically valuable. Which are the most inimitable, durable, appropriable, non-substitutable and superior to the competition?

Then apply the approach we used in Chapter 5:

■ Identify strategically valuable resources.

■ Appraise them:
  – Assess their relative importance
  – Assess your relative strengths
  – Bring the appraisal together.

■ Develop strategy implications.

Collis and Montgomery suggest that you should invest in strategically valuable resources for sustainable competitive advantage, perhaps in three ways:

■ Invest in those you have – for example, Disney reinvesting in animation.

■ Leverage those you have – for example, Disney leveraging its brand name into retailing and publishing.

■ Upgrade those you should have – for example, Intel moving into consumer branding with 'Intel Inside'.

A strategy that combines the two different perspectives, internally focused capabilities and external awareness of the dynamic industry context and competitive environment, can be powerful.

Essential tip

By all means use the resource-based view of strategy for your firm, but preferably in conjunction with Porter-esque industry/ market analysis, as with Collis and Montgomery's strategically valuable resources.

Essential tool

Building core competences

What are your firm's core competences?

Hamel and Prahalad in their 1994 book, *Competing for the Future*, believed that there was much more to corporate strategy than just portfolio planning. Corporate HQ had a major role to play in areas such as developing strengths in key operational processes (termed 'core competences') and conveying a sense of vision throughout the firm ('strategic intent').

Instead of the downsizing or re-engineering prevalent at the time, companies should be 'reinventing their industry' or 'regenerating their strategy'. They proposed a new, ambitious strategy paradigm.

They define a core competence as an 'integrated bundle of skills and technologies'. It represents the 'sum of learning across individual skill sets in individual organisational units'. It is unlikely to reside in a single individual or small team, and may not reside in a single business unit.

Core competences in financial services, for example, are quoted as relationship management, transaction processing, risk management, foreign exchange, financial engineering, trading skills, investment management, tele-service and customer information capture.

They see the key to competing for the future as the building, deploying, protecting and defending of your core competences.

You should ask these questions of your businesses:

- What is the opportunity to improve your position by better leveraging your current core competences?

■ What new competences will you need to build to protect and defend your franchise?

■ What new businesses could you create by redeploying or recombining your existing core competences?

■ What new core competences would you need to build to participate in the most exciting businesses of the future?

The more distinctive, the more unique, the more defensible is your core competence, the more value it has.

How can you strengthen your core competences and thereby build value?

Essential example

UU U-turn

'I want to break free' was topping the charts around the time that the other Queen's government was contemplating the privatisation of the UK's water utilities. That philosophy seemed to have stayed with the water company bosses by the time they privatised in 1989.

They wanted to break free from regulation. They felt enchained by the regulator, Ofwat, in areas such as franchised territory, service quality, capital expenditure and, of course, pricing. They yearned for the liberty of non-regulated businesses, which they were empowered by Ofwat to pursue only under separate corporate structures.

They believed that their new shareholders would not be satisfied by the level of returns to be gained from sticking to the slow, steady, unexciting water business – shareholders of a publicly quoted stock would expect the higher returns commensurate with non-regulated businesses.

This was a fallacy and too often an expensive one. Shareholders can do their own diversification – they can hold stock in a low-risk, low-return water company as well as in non-regulated, higher-return, higher-risk companies.

The diversification strategy would have been valid only if the water company could have brought something to the non-regulated business, or vice versa, that would have enhanced its value – in other words, the creation of synergy. 'Better management' was hardly likely to be a transferable skill – the water company bosses had been working in the public sector for years and most had little experience of working in the public glare of a PLC.

They nevertheless went on a spending spree, setting up international operations or making acquisitions in overseas water companies or in sectors such as waste management, engineering or other utilities. Many international sorties, whether acquisitions or major contracts, led to large write-offs, including Anglian Water in Norway, Thames Water in Egypt and North West Water in Thailand.

The largest water company, North West Water, based in the wettest part of Britain, diversified more than most. Five years after privatisation it merged with Norweb, the main electricity distributor in north-west England, aiming for synergies in areas such as customer acquisition and service, metering, billing and other administration. Indeed, the newly named United Utilities soon carved out these services into a new venture, Vertex, designed to be an outsourcer for third-party business.

Over the years it diversified into international water companies, in a joint venture with Bechtel in the Philippines and Australia, it acquired businesses in the industrial water and wastewater treatment sector and it invested in gas distribution and business telephony – while withdrawing from the retail electricity market.

Towards the end of the 2000s, the company had a wholesale rethink of corporate strategy. It did a U-turn. It decided to re-focus on its water business, now deemed to be core. It sold off its electricity distribution assets, returning £1.5 billion to shareholders, and sold Vertex too – thus reversing the rationale for the initial merger between North West Water and Norweb itself.

It also sold off its other non-core assets, including all the international ventures and shareholdings in gas and telecommunications. Disposals of non-core assets raised £600m.

These realisations were substantial. But whether or not shareholder value at United Utilities was created or destroyed by this process over two decades of merger and diversification, followed by demerger and concentration, *in comparison to alternative strategies for the allocation of scarce shareholder funds*, is open to doubt and would require detailed investigation.

Suffice to say that the original strategy of breaking free from regulated business has now been thoroughly reversed, by United Utilities and most other water companies. The regulated business is no longer regarded as a Cinderella. Focus on the core, Chris Zook-style, has become the prevailing philosophy. Non-core businesses have been axed. To return to the Queen theme of the start, 'another one bites the dust'.

Corporate strategic risks and opportunities

What are the 'big' risks and opportunities associated with your chosen corporate strategy – those which are at least reasonably likely to occur and with reasonable impact upon occurrence?

They may be the risk of enticing only a couple of interested parties when you sell off an unwanted business, or, conversely, the opportunity of acquiring a business for a price below market value due to you approaching a vendor 'below the radar' (that is, without the business being put through an auction process).

Or it may be the risk of your investing to build up company-wide capability in a key business process only to find that technology has moved on.

These big risks and opportunities concerning your corporate strategy will be blended with those of market demand, competition and business strategy in the next chapter and assessed for balance and viability.

Essential case study

Extramural Ltd Strategic Review, 2013

Chapter 8: Corporate strategy

Richard and Jane Davies have developed what they firmly believe to be a winning strategy for their school activity tours business – see Chapter 7. They will differentiate Extramural as the learning-cum-activity provider par excellence by investing in ICT suite and language lab facilities and by carefully focused marketing.

▶

Meanwhile they will implement a complete cultural change in all aspects of customer service to upgrade the customer experience over time to best-in-class.

But what of Extramural's other two businesses? These were analysed by the Davieses in just as much detail as for school activity tours, but left out of the write-up of Chapter 7 due to space constraints. In summary, the findings were, for educational tours:

- Good-quality offering, respected in the market, perceived to be there or thereabouts in terms of efficiency, delivery, customer service and quality of guides as for market leaders, STL and EduTours.

- Low market share, 8% compared to STL's dominant 45%, gives Extramural little clout with travel and hospitality companies, making it cost uncompetitive.

- A me-too operator, with no evident differentiation enabling any premium on price, Extramural yields a contribution margin of 41%, compared to STL's estimated 56%.

- Extramural is sub-scale and would need to either specialise in a niche or grow through acquisition to improve margins towards STL's levels.

And for day camps:

- Extramural is a recent new entrant, with just six camps and 5% market share so far, well behind Ultra Camps, KoolKamps and Monkeys, which share two-thirds of the market between them.

- Despite efforts to persuade the customer otherwise, there is little differentiation between any of the players – the range of activities in an Ultra Camp will be little different from that in Extramural, with each player boasting mainly lively, enthusiastic and youthful instructors and minders.

- So far, so similar to Extramural's position in educational tours, but the economics are very different – this is a business where economies of scale are limited to marketing, much of which is local and inexpensive, and administration, but emphatically not to purchasing; this enables hundreds of small operators, from one-site activity camps to cricket camps, cookery camps to scout camps, pottery camps to drama camps, to survive and often to thrive.

■ Unlike in educational tours, where the market is mature, this is a market growing at around 10% per year, driven by steady growth in families with two working parents, parental aspirations and the steep and rising cost of childcare, especially during the summer months.

■ But Extramural is again sub-scale and would need to grow by acquisition to make any significant dent in the marketplace.

Richard and Jane start to draw up a strategic position chart for the company as a whole, assessing each of the three businesses by market attractiveness and competitive position. First, however, they must rank the three businesses by market attractiveness, as follows (see Table 8.1):

■ Day camps is the most attractive, with strong growth, high profitability and low risk.

■ School activity tours comes next, with a big market, profitability almost as high, but higher demand risk.

■ Then it's educational tours, with low growth and tough competition for any other than the two leading players.

Table 8.1 **Extramural Ltd: market attractiveness of the three businesses**

Criteria	School activity tours	Educational tours	Day camps
Market size	4	3	2
Market growth	2	2	4
Competitive intensity	3	2	3
Industry profitability	4	3	5
Market risk	2	3	4
Overall attractiveness	**3.0**	**2.6**	**3.6**

Key to rating: 1 = Unattractive, 3 = Reasonably attractive, 5 = Highly attractive
[For competitive intensity, remember that the more intense the competition, the *less* attractive the market. Likewise for market risk: the riskier the market, the *less* attractive]

These ratings give the Davieses their y-axis values. They have already worked out competitive position ratings for the x-axis, so they now complete the strategic position chart – see Figure 8.2. They use the same GE/McKinsey chart as used in Chapter

▶

6 to assess strategic position in each business, but this time the bubbles are businesses, not segments.

Extramural's strategic position seems clear at first glance. The school activity tour business is well placed, with room for improvement, while the day camp business may have promise – a tenable competitive position in an attractive market. But the educational tours business doesn't look good – a tenable competitive position in a relatively less attractive market.

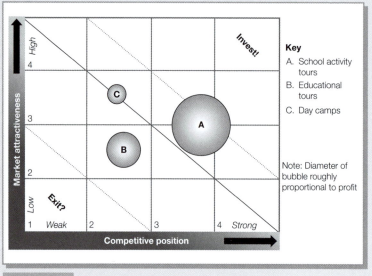

Figure 8.2   **Extramural Ltd: strategic position**

The Davieses feel they may already know the answer but, to be sure, they seek a second opinion. They look to The Boston Consulting Group growth share matrix and plot the three businesses on that (see Figure 8.3).

None of the three businesses looks particularly happy here. At a market share relative to the leader (ActivTours) of 0.68 and operating in a slow-growing market, even the school activity tours business comes out as a dog – though nowhere near as canine as the educational tours business, with a market share of 0.15 relative to the leader (STL) and a similarly lethargic market.

Day camps, however, is a question mark. Despite Extramural's late entry into the market and a mere 0.20 market share relative

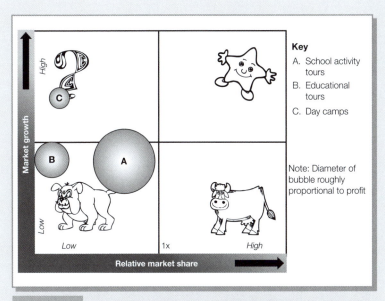

Figure 8.3   **Extramural Ltd: growth share business portfolio**

Source: Adapted from the BCG Portfolio Matrix from the Product Portfolio Matrix
© 1970, The Boston Consulting Group

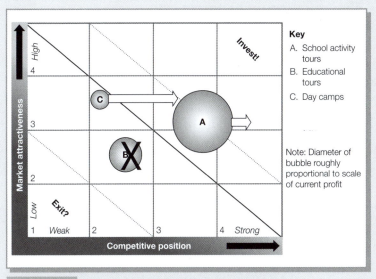

Figure 8.4   **Extramural Ltd: strategic repositioning**

to the leader (Ultra Camps), it is a business facing a fast-growing market, thus escaping the nomenclature of dog.

The corporate strategy the Davieses should pursue now stands out starkly (see Figure 8.4):

- Exit from educational tours
- Use proceeds to invest in school activity tours, nudging that business from quasi-dog to cash cow . . .
- . . . and grow by acquisition in day camps.

But there is one further check the Davieses must do before they contemplate implementing this corporate strategy. How interlinked are these businesses? If one is axed, will that affect competitiveness in another? What are the inter-business synergies?

The Davieses now see in retrospect that it was a strategic error to have moved into educational tours. It was an opportunistic move. A friend had suggested that Jane meet another friend who was looking for a buyer for her educational tours business. The deal had been cosy, the price good, the business taken on seamlessly.

But the synergies with the school activity tour business had been minimal. There was limited overlap in marketing to primary schools, with most educational tours abroad, whether a trip to the Normandy battle sites or to Pompeii, sold to secondary schools or colleges. And very little overlap in purchasing, with most travel suppliers to educational tours, other than coach operators, not participating in school activity tours.

The truth is that Extramural is probably not the best parent for the educational tour business (see Goold, Campbell and Alexander's essential tool, Creating Parenting Value). The business might be better homed under one of the two market leaders, or a fellow mid-sized player looking to become larger, or a foreign entrant.

Extramural thus has every chance of realising a good price for its educational tours business. A good corporate finance adviser should be able to engineer an active auction between prospective trade and private equity buyers.

The proceeds from this divestment can be invested in Extramural's remaining two businesses – initially into financing the new strategy developed by the Davieses for the school activity tour business and the balance, topped up as necessary by tapping Extramural's underexploited debt capacity, in acquiring a sizeable day camp operator.

Day camps is a business that offers significant synergies with the school activity tour business. All school activity tour operators fill their rooms with ease during much of term time, but find it more difficult to fill their summer residential tour capacity. Day camp customers offer them a temporarily captive market and a database ripe for picking, and likewise vice versa, yielding tangible cross-selling synergies. Likewise there are marketing synergies between the businesses, given that both day and residential customers tend to access the same media.

The Davieses believe they have developed a robust corporate strategy. But there is one more step: how risky is this strategy? That is for Chapter 9.

Essential checklist on bridging the corporate strategy gap

■ Optimise your corporate portfolio by investing in certain businesses, holding in others, entering new ones and divesting those businesses where your competitive position is poor and which address unattractive markets.

■ Check whether you come to the same conclusions using The Boston Consulting Group growth share matrix.

■ Ensure that you create value from any planned mergers, acquisitions or alliances. Pay no more for the target than its stand-alone value plus the value of the synergies, suitably discounted to temper any elements of 'deal fever'.

■ Consider whether any of your businesses would be better parented by another company – and, if so, what that company might be willing to pay for the business to gain control.

■ Invest in those company-wide resources and capabilities (or 'competences') which are strategically valuable and will give your company a sustainable competitive advantage.

■ Assess the most important risks and opportunities associated with your corporate strategy.

9

Addressing risk and opportunity

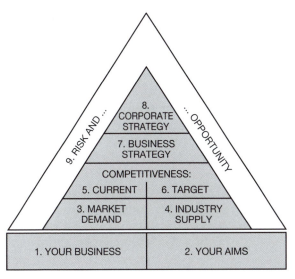

> The biggest risk is not taking any risk ... In a world that is changing really quickly, the only strategy that is guaranteed to fail is not taking risks.
>
> *Mark Zuckerberg*

In this chapter

- Reviewing the plan in a market context
- Appraising opportunity versus risk
  - Essential tool: Expected value and sensitivity analysis

Strategy development and strategic due diligence are as two peas in the same pod. They feed off the same nutrients – market demand, industry supply and competitive advantage.

They are mirror images of one another. In strategy development you assemble the micro-economic and competitive position information and conjure up a means of creating sustainable competitive advantage. In strategic due diligence you review that strategy in the context of the same micro-economic and competitive information.

Strategic due diligence ('SDD') is used primarily in mergers and acquisitions. Without a thorough assessment of the market, industry and competitive risks and opportunities facing the target, the acquirer runs the risk of paying too much to gain control. The penalties of inadequate due diligence can be catastrophic – ask the then shareholders of RBS (or Lloyds TSB) what a terrific idea it was to have bought ABN AMRO (or HBoS).

But it can also be used constructively as a check on the strategy development process. Think of the latter as the manufacturing process on the shop floor of a one-off, made-to-order, very large item of capital equipment. SDD then is the quality control unit, tasked with verifying that the output has emerged as it should.

This equipment, this strategy, should be fit for purpose – it should be what the market is prepared to pay for and it should stand out from the competition. If not, it should be resubmitted to the shop floor for final adjustments.

Let SDD fine-tune your strategy.

SDD seeks the answer to one basic and one supplementary question.

The basic question is: Is this firm likely to achieve its plan over the next few years? And the supplementary: Do the opportunities to beat plan outweigh the risks of not achieving it?

You will deal with the supplementary question in a while. To address the basic question, you need to review your plan in a market context.

Reviewing the plan in a market context

Throughout this strategy development process you have been urged to frame your strategy in the context of the micro-economy in which you operate. Now is the time to see how well you have done – to use the Market Contextual Plan Review. This consists of two parts – setting revenues in the context of market demand and setting margins in the context of industry competition.

Table 9.1 Market contextual plan review

Product/Market segments	Revenues (£000)	Market demand growth (%/year)	Competitive position (0–5)	Plan revenues (£000)	Plan revenue growth (%/year)	How Achievable?	Likely revenues (£000)
	This year	Next three years	Next three tears	In three years	Next three years		In three years
1	2	3	4	5	6	7	8
A							
B							
C							
Others							
Total							

Start with your revenue forecasts. You need to check that these are compatible with your assumptions on market demand growth and future competitive position.

For each of your businesses draw up a table as in Table 9.1 with at least eight columns (as shown in the table) and possibly (preferably, unless you find too many columns confusing) 14 (the extra six are listed in *italics* below), as follows:

1 Main product/market segments

Revenues

2 Revenues in latest year, and possibly also:
- *Budgeted revenues for next year*
- *Revenues in previous year*
- *Revenues in year before that*
- *Revenue growth (% per year) over last three years*
- *Market demand growth in nominal terms over last three years*

Market context

3 Market demand growth forecasts in nominal terms over next three years (note that there is no entry in the bottom row, since you are forecasting by specific segment – also for column 4)

4 Your firm's average competitive position rating (0–5) in that segment over the next three years, or current rating in this column and in the next:

■   *Likely rating in three years' time, showing impact of strategy*

Revenue forecasts

5   Your firm's planned revenues in three years' time

6   Your firm's planned revenue growth rate over the next three
years

A backer's perspective

7   How achievable? – look at planned revenues in the context of
market dynamics from the perspective of a backer (and finally
how achievable the overall revenues number is for the business
in the bottom row)

8   Your firm's more likely revenues – what a backer would be more
prepared to finance.

You have looked at your emergent strategy and plan from a top-down
perspective, that of a potential backer doing SDD on your company.

Your backer will be looking for inconsistencies. In general, your
revenue forecasts in each segment should be consistent with:

■   Your track record of revenue growth

■   Market demand prospects

■   Your competitive position, now and over the next few years.

Any inconsistencies need justification.

If your track record in a segment is good and your competitive position
strong, and poised to get stronger, your backer would expect your
revenue forecasts, *ceteris paribus*, to exceed those of market demand,
to gain market share.

If, however, your track record is not good and/or your competitive
position is currently only tenable and your revenue forecasts still
exceed those of market demand, your backer would be concerned at
this apparent inconsistency and would need to know why.

Can your strategy, designed to strengthen that competitive position,
support such a forecast? Is it robust?

Table 9.2 Market contextual margin review

Segments	Revs (£000) This year	Profit margin (%) This year	Profit (£000) This year	Competitive intensity (L/M/H) Now	Next three years	Plan profit margin (%) In three years	How achievable?	Likely profit margin (%) In three years	Likely revs (£000) In three years	Likely profit (£000) In three years
1	2	3	4	5	6	7	8	9	10	11
A										
B										
C										
Others										
Total										

The second element of the Market Contextual Plan Review concerns margins. Draw up another table with 11 columns (see Table 9.2), as follows:

1 The same product/market segments

Profits

2 Revenues in latest year again

3 Profit margin in latest year (preferably contribution margin but, if unavailable at that level of segmentation, gross margin will do)

4 Profit in latest year, contribution preferably (or gross profit) = column 2 × column 3

Industry competition

5 Competitive intensity in this segment currently (low/medium/ high) – from Porter's five forces analysis (see Chapter 4)

6 Competitive intensity over the next three years – is it likely to augment, subside or stay flat?

Profit forecasts

7 Planned profit margin in three years' time

A backer's perspective

8 How achievable? Look at planned margin in the context of industry competition dynamics from the perspective of a backer (and finally how achievable the overall margin is for the business in the bottom row)

9 Your firm's more likely profit margin – what a backer would be more prepared to finance

10 Your likely revenues – from Table 9.1

11 Your likely profit = column 9 × column 10.

Again, through the eyes of a prospective backer, you should be looking for consistency. If your forecasts show flat margins within a context of little anticipated change in competitive intensity, they are consistent; likewise if they show rising margins in an industry where competition is easing.

But if your forecasts show rising margins in an industry where competition is getting tougher, they are inconsistent. They are not necessarily wrong, but they do need justification. Reasons are manifold but may include:

- Improved purchasing
- Higher utilisation
- Greater productivity
- Product line rationalisation
- Economies of scale (see Chapter 4)
- Experience curve effects (Chapter 7)
- Business process redesign
- Outsourcing
- Belt tightening.

But they need to be coherent, consistent and convincing.

Essential tip

Use strategic due diligence and market contextual plan review when you need to fine-tune your strategy. The aim should be that the strategy emerges sufficiently robust to withstand the forensic cross-examination of a specialist strategic due diligence house engaged by a diligent private equity client.

Appraising opportunity versus risk

Strategic due diligence (SDD) seeks to address the balance of risk and opportunity in your strategic plan. It looks for risks and opportunities in four main areas:

▨ *Demand risk* – how risky is future market demand?

▨ *Competition risk* – how risky is future competitive intensity?

▨ *Competitive position risk* – how risky is your firm's strategy, both business and corporate, and future competitive position?

▨ *Business plan risk* – how risky is your firm's plan?

Each of these areas of risk and opportunity goes towards making up a risk jigsaw, as shown in Figure 9.1. SDD seeks to put together the four pieces of the jigsaw and assess the overall balance of risk and opportunity.

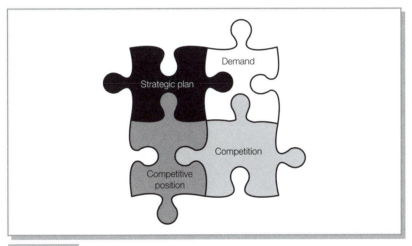

Figure 9.1 The risk jigsaw of strategic due diligence

You have already assembled all the raw material for the risk analysis on your firm. At the end of Chapters 3, 4, 7 and 8, you pulled out the 'big' risks and opportunities associated with, respectively, market demand, industry competition, business strategy and corporate strategy – with 'big' being defined as having at least a reasonable likelihood of occurrence or at least a reasonable impact on value.

You are now ready for these key risks and opportunities to be analysed in a 'Suns & Clouds chart'.

I first created the Suns & Clouds chart in the early 1990s. Since then I've seen it reproduced in various forms in reports by my consulting competitors. They say imitation is the sincerest form of flattery, but I still kick myself that I didn't copyright it back then!

The reason it keeps getting pinched is that it works. It manages to encapsulate in one chart conclusions on the relative importance of all the main strategic issues. It shows, diagrammatically and visually, whether the opportunities surpass the risks, or vice versa. In short, in one chart, it tells you whether your strategy is backable – or not.

The chart (Figure 9.2) forces you to view each risk (and opportunity) from two perspectives: how likely it is to happen, and how big an impact it would have if it did. You don't need to quantify the impact, but instead you need to have some idea of the notional, *relative* impact of each issue on the value of the firm.

In the chart, risks are represented as clouds, opportunities as suns. For each risk (and opportunity), you need to place it in the appropriate position on the chart taking into account both its likelihood and its impact.

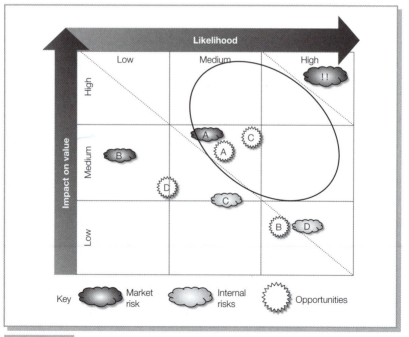

Figure 9.2 The sun and clouds chart

The Suns & Clouds chart tells you two main things about how backable is your strategy: whether there are any *extraordinary* risks (or opportunities), and whether the overall *balance* of risk and opportunity is favourable.

Extraordinary risk

Take a look at the top right-hand corner of the chart. There's a heavy thundercloud in there, with two exclamation marks. That's a risk that is both very likely *and* very big. It's a showstopper risk. If you find one of them, your strategy is unbackable.

The closer a cloud gets to that thundercloud, the worse news it is. Risks that hover around the diagonal (from the top left to the bottom right corners) can be handled, as long as they are balanced by opportunities. But as soon as a cloud starts creeping towards that thundercloud, for example to around where opportunity C is placed, that's when you should start to worry.

But imagine a bright shining sun in that spot where the thundercloud is. That's terrific news, and you'll have suitors clambering over each other to back you.

The balance

In general there's no showstopper risk. The main purpose of the Suns & Clouds chart will then be to present the *balance* of risk and opportunity. Do the opportunities surpass the risks? Given the overall picture, are the suns more favourably placed than the clouds? Or do the clouds overshadow the suns?

The way to assess a Suns & Clouds chart is to look first at the general area above the diagonal and in the direction of the thundercloud. This is the area covered in Figure 9.2 by the parabola. Any risk (or opportunity) there is worthy of note: it's at least reasonably likely to occur *and* would have at least a reasonable impact.

Those risks and opportunities below the diagonal are less important. Either they're of low to medium likelihood *and* of low to medium impact, or they're not big enough, or not likely enough, to be of major concern.

Take a look at the pattern of suns and clouds in your chart around the area of the parabola. The closer each sun and cloud is to the thundercloud, the more important it is. If the pattern of suns seems better placed than the pattern of clouds, your strategy may be backable.

In Figure 9.2 there are two clouds and two suns above the diagonal.

But risk D lies outside the parabola. The best placed is opportunity B. Risk A and opportunity A more or less balance each other out, likewise other risks and opportunities. Opportunity B seems distinctly clear of the pack. The opportunities seem to surpass the risks. The business looks backable.

One of the best features of the Suns & Clouds chart is that it can be made dynamic. If the balance of risk and opportunity shown on the chart is unfavourable, you may be able to do something about it – and illuminate your action on the chart.

For every risk, there are mitigating factors. Many, including those relating to market demand and competition (the darker clouds in Figure 9.2), will be beyond your control. Those relating to your firm's competitive position, however, are within your power to influence. They may indeed be an integral part of your emergent strategy.

Likewise, your strategy may improve the likelihood of achieving a key opportunity on the chart, thereby shifting the sun to the right.

Risk mitigation or opportunity enhancement in the Suns & Clouds chart can be illuminated with arrows and target signs. They'll show where your firm should aim for and remind you that it's a target. Your strategy should improve the overall balance of risk and opportunity in your firm.

You can use the Suns & Clouds chart in so many situations. It was designed for SDD purposes in transactions such as acquisitions, alliances and investments, but it is just as useful in project appraisal, in strategy review (as here) or even in career development and change. It might even have been useful in deciding whether or not to have backed Britney (see the essential case study).

What about highly improbable but potentially catastrophic risks, you might ask? And those which seem explicable, even justifiable, only in retrospect, termed Black Swans by Nassim Nicholas Taleb – like the 2008 financial meltdown? The chart deals with them too.

In the autumn of 2001, my colleagues and I were advising a client on whether to invest in a company involved in airport operations. After the first week of work, we produced an interim report and a first-cut Suns & Clouds chart. In the top left-hand corner box, we placed a risk entitled 'major air incident'. We were thinking of a serious air crash that might lead to the prolonged grounding of a common class of aircraft. It seemed unlikely, but it would have a very large impact if it happened.

'9/11' came just a few days later. We never envisaged anything so devastating, so inconceivably evil, but at least we had alerted our client to the extreme risks involved in the air industry. The deal was renegotiated and completed successfully.

Essential tip

Don't worry if your Suns & Clouds chart doesn't make that much sense initially. This chart changes with further thought and discussion. *Always*. Arguably its greatest virtue is its stimulus to discussion. It provokes amendment.

Remember, you cannot be exact in this chart. Nor do you need to be. It is a pictorial representation of risk and opportunity, designed to give you a *feel* for the balance of risk and opportunity in your strategy.

Essential tool: Expected value and sensitivity analysis

Expected value is the nominal value of an order multiplied by the probability of winning it. It is the real value of an order to you.

This concept can be immensely useful in forecasting, especially if yours is a 'lumpy' business with few, sporadic, large orders – such as in automotive components (where the supplier either wins or doesn't win a place on a programme which can last for years), capital equipment, outsourcing or management consulting.

Each prospective order can be probability-weighted and the resultant expected values totted up to yield an overall expected value total.

This total then becomes the base-case order forecast, against which you can apply sensitivity testing.

Suppose your firm has existing orders totalling 1000 units and 10 prospective new orders, ranging from 30 to 300 units, over the next three years – see Table 9.3.

One commonly found way of forecasting future orders would be to take different scenarios – a downside case, where only the

| Table 9.3 | Expected value: an example |

Orders	Y1	Y2	Y3	Probability	Downside Case Y3	Expected Value Y3
Existing:	1000	1050	1100	100%	1100	1100
New:						
A	40	40	40	90%	40	36
B	50	50	50	80%	50	40
C	30	30	30	45%	0	13.5
D	80	80	80	20%	0	16
E		180	180	60%	180	108
F		30	30	55%	30	16.5
G		40	40	40%	0	16
H			60	30%	0	18
I			90	70%	90	63
J			300	10%	0	30
Total	**1200**	**1500**	**2000**		**1490**	**1457**

more likely orders come in, and an upside case, where they all come in. The base case would then split the difference.

Thus in this example the downside case (taking only new orders where probability is greater than 50%) would give total orders in Year 3 of 1490 units. The upside case gives 2000 units, so the base case would be 1745 (half-way).

But this greatly overestimates likely future orders. The largest one, for 300 units, has just a 10% probability. It is excluded from the downside case but included in the upside case, therefore partly included in the base case – with an *implied* probability of 50%, when in reality it should be just 10%. The second-largest order, for 180 units, is included in both the downside and upside cases, hence has an implied probability in the base case of 100%, when it should be just 60%.

Far more realistic for future planning purposes is to apply individual probabilities to each individual new order to obtain expected values, the total of which should be a more usable base case – in this case, 1457 units in Year 3.

That should be the base around which sensitivity testing can proceed. Sensitivity analysis is another time-tested tool for testing for uncertainty of inputs and analysing the impact on outputs. Values of selected inputs can be varied, typically by 5–10%, to assess impact on output.

In this case, having established a base case, appropriate sensitivity tests could be:

- With Order E – giving total orders of 1529 units (note that the base case rises by only 72, the difference between 60% and 100% of 180)
- Without Order E – 1349 units
- With Order J – 1727 units
- Without Order J – 1427 units
- With Orders E and J – 1799 units
- Without Orders E and J – 1319 units.

The impact of these sensitivity tests on sales, P&L and cash flow can then be measured and appropriate flexibility built into the firm's operations to be able to handle each outcome competently.

The most common type of sensitivity tests come from varying key parameters such as:

- Sales volume forecasts up or down by 5–10%
- Unit pricing forecasts up or down by 2–3%
- Labour costs up 5%
- Capex up 10%.

Again, the impact of these varied inputs can be evaluated on the key financial and operational outputs and appropriate action taken.

Expected value is most appropriately used where there are yes/ no moments which can have a major impact on your business. It is less useful in businesses where there are large numbers of customers, such as in consumer goods or services, but even there it can be used on the revenue side to allow for the success of individual segment initiatives or on the cost side for major 'lumpy items', such as lease renewal.

Sensitivity analysis should be used in all investment appraisals, whether expected values are used or not.

Essential tip

Take care with the individual probabilities. It is human nature to overinflate expectations. Over-optimism may help in team motivation but is most unhelpful in business planning.

Essential example

Britney does it again

Who do you think was the highest-paid woman in the music industry in 2012? According to *Forbes* magazine, it was not 1950s throwback Katy Perry, in at number five, nor the whacky Lady Gaga or the raunchy Rihanna, not even the runner-up, country crossover singer-songwriter, Taylor Swift. The phenomenon that is Beyoncé, with astonishing vocal range, stunning looks and Tina Turner-esque command of the stage, was not even in the top five.

No, it was the schoolgirl sensation from the late 1990s, back at the top with $68m.

Britney stormed onto the music scene in December 1998 with *Baby One More Time*. The voice was good enough, as was the song, but it was the positioning of this 17-year-old that sealed the deal, with the video designed overtly to fuel the fantasies of every schoolboy and the aspirations of every schoolgirl – including my two. She became their goddess and, as soon as Britney brought out her first fragrance, Santa duly obliged.

History may tell us that this video marked a seminal moment in the sad but inexorable process of the sexualisation of schoolchildren, but it did the trick for Britney. She became the bestselling teenage artist ever and by 2002 *Forbes* magazine was rating her as the world's most powerful celebrity.

But in early 2004 came the first signs that something was amiss. She married a childhood sweetheart in Las Vegas, then annulled the marriage within three days. She attended the Kabbalah sect of her role model, Madonna. She became engaged to a dancer and opened up their lives in a three-month reality show. They had two children, but sadly divorced within two years.

She became in her own words an 'emotional wreck'. She partied heavily with the likes of Paris Hilton, flirting with paparazzi and flagrantly displaying her absence of underwear. She shaved off all her hair. She checked in and out of drug rehabilitation centres. She lost custody of her children to her ex-husband. By early 2008 she was hospitalised and put under the conservatorship of her father.

If you were a music industry mogul in mid-2008, would you have backed Britney? The risks were huge. She had been a teen star like none other, but that was yesterday. At 27 she was passé, troubled and unreliable. Her looks had lost their freshness, her body had turned maternal, her voice remained unexceptional. How could she compete with a Beyoncé?

Let's look at her Suns & Clouds – see Figure 9.3.

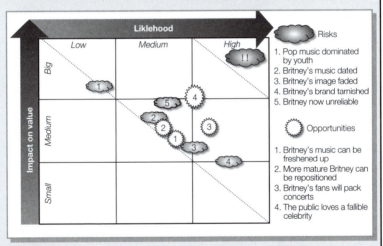

Figure 9.3   **Would you have backed Britney in 2008?**

It wouldn't have looked too good. Risks and opportunities seem more or less balanced out – with Britney's dated music, fading image, tarnished brand and unreliable character balanced by opportunities to freshen up the music, reposition her as more mature and rely on the legion of diehard fans to show up when her concert comes to town, again like my daughters!

But one opportunity steals the show. The public loves a fallible celebrity. And any news is good news. As long as she could pull herself together, and perform when required, countering that risk #5, that opportunity, sun #4, should shine through to success.

And, yes, four years later, oops, she did it again and hit us, baby, one more time.

Essential case study

Extramural Ltd Strategic Review, 2013

Chapter 9: Risk and opportunity

Richard and Jane Davies have developed what they perceive to be a sound corporate strategy (see Chapter 8), a key element of which is a robust business strategy in school activity tours (Chapter 7).

But what are the risks of such a strategy? How will they fare in relation to the opportunities before Extramural? What will the balance between risk and opportunity be like?

They start by revisiting each section of the Strategy Pyramid, pulling out the most important risks and opportunities from each section. Under forecasting market demand, for example, they refer to Table 3.5, which rated each of the major risks and opportunities against the likelihood of their occurrence and their impact on value should they occur. Likewise, for the other sections, whether on industry competition or business strategy, they have compiled similar tables as they went along (not shown in this book).

The donkey work already done, all they need to do now is transpose those risks and opportunities with the most impact onto a Suns & Clouds chart – see Figure 9.4.

The Davieses rub their eyes. They see before them a hugely encouraging chart. Six main risks have been highlighted, but most of these are of low probability, even if of high impact, such as the risk of either the Government or another teacher union turning against the concept of school activity tours during term time.

The one risk to emerge with a medium/high probability and a medium impact is that of competitive response from ActivTours to

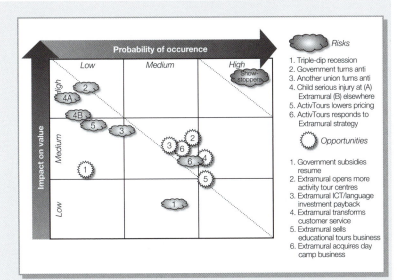

Figure 9.4 | **Extramural Ltd: risks and opportunities**

Extramural's strategy of differentiation (into a learning-cum-activity tour specialist) in school activity tours.

But this risk is surrounded and completely outshone by a host of opportunities, including Extramural acquiring more activity centres (the most promising of all opportunities, given the known economies of scale), investing in ICT suites and language labs, transforming its customer service, selling its educational tours business for a good price and acquiring a day camp business.

The Davieses are hugely fired up by this chart. They have surely found the strategy, both corporate and business, to guide them into a position in five years' time when they can move on to another chapter of their lives. And they will do so in the knowledge that they have done their very best for themselves, their family, their employees and, perhaps above all, those many thousands of small, grinning faces it has been their privilege to serve over a quarter of a century.

Essential checklist on addressing risk and opportunity

- Carry out a market contextual plan review on your sales and profit forecasts.

- Are your sales forecasts for each segment consistent with your track record, your market demand prospects and your evolving competitive position?

- Are your margin forecasts consistent with your track record, trends in competitive intensification and your planned performance improvement measures?

- Pull out all the 'big' risks and opportunities relating to market demand, competitive intensity, business strategy and corporate strategy. Assess them in a Suns & Clouds chart for likelihood of occurrence and impact on value should they occur.

- Are there any extraordinary risks? If so, take remedial action to avoid or mitigate them.

- What is the balance of risk and opportunity?

- If the opportunities outshine the risks, your strategy seems promising. If the risks overshadow the opportunities, it's back to the drawing board.

Strategic planning

10

The strategic plan

> In real life, strategy is actually very straightforward. You pick a
> general direction and implement like hell.
>
> *Jack Welch*

In this chapter

- Strategy + Business Plan = Strategic Plan
- Contents of a strategic plan
- Reviewing the plan

Part One was the easy part. Now for the real work.

You have a strategy. Now you need to put it into effect.

Napoleon Bonaparte put it best: 'The art of war is simple; everything is a matter of execution'.

The first step in execution is the strategic plan.

Strategy + Business Plan = Strategic Plan

A strategic plan is the first step beyond strategy development, the first step into strategy implementation.

It is no longer a helicopter view of the direction of movement. It becomes a ground-level view on moving.

But it is not a daily or weekly set of actions to be taken. That would be too detailed – more appropriate to project planning and implementation.

A strategic plan leads to a high-level set of actions to be taken to put a strategy into effect.

In particular, a strategic plan focuses on resource deployment – cash, human and physical. It thus includes a detailed investment plan.

You can think of a strategic plan in these terms: it includes the formulation of strategy as well as the resource allocation implications found in a business plan.

Thus: Strategy + Business Plan = Strategic Plan.

This is not to plug this book's companion guide, *The FT Essential Guide to Writing a Business Plan: How to Win Backing to Start Up or Grow Your Business*, but there are areas where the two books overlap importantly and other areas which are more pertinent to one or the other. Together they combine all that is needed in strategic planning.

-

To see this, let's look at selected chapters from each book:

Developing a Business Strategy	Writing a Business Plan
	1. Preparation
1. The business	2. The business (including
2. Goals and objectives	goals and objectives)
3. Market demand	3. Market demand
4. Competition	4. Competition
5. Competitive advantage	5. Strategy
6. Strategic gap	
7. Bridging the gap: business	
8. Bridging the gap: corporate	
	6. Resources
	7. Financials and forecasts
9. Risk and opportunity	8. Risk and opportunity

Common to both books are the critical analysis of the firm's micro-economic environment (market demand and competition) and the concluding wrap-up on risk and opportunity.

Developing a Business Strategy delves deeper (see Chapters 5–8) on strategy, while *Writing a Business Plan* gives only a cursory summary of the strategy development process.

The meat of *Writing a Business Plan* resides in the deployment of resources – management, marketing, operations and capital expenditure – and the financials and forecasts – market-driven sales forecasts, competition-driven margin forecasts, funding options, P&L, cash flow and balance sheet historics and forecasts. A business plan is typically written to entice a backer. They need to know in detail how much that strategy is going to cost, and with what likely returns, downsides and upsides.

A strategic plan needs to incorporate all this – the development of strategy, the resource implications, an investment plan, the financials, the risk and sensitivity analysis – plus a bit more, a high-level action plan.

Contents of a strategic plan

The above section has pointed the way towards the content of a strategic plan. It goes without saying that any template should be treated with caution. Each organisation is different, each faces its own challenges. Some sections may be less relevant, others may need further extension. New sections may need to be added.

But here is a basic template:

- Introduction and summary of team, timetable and strategy development process
- Summary of conclusions
- The business today (Chapter 1 of this book)
- Goals and objectives (Chapter 2)
- Market demand (Chapter 3)
- Industry competition (Chapter 4)
- Competitive advantage (Chapter 5) – and how this may change over time
- The strategic gap (Chapter 6) – and how identified
- Business strategy (Chapter 7) – and why selected over other options
- Corporate strategy (Chapter 8) – and why selected over other options
- Resource deployment – the implications of the selected strategy
  - Management
  - Marketing
  - Operations
  - Personnel
  - Capital expenditure
- Financials and forecasts – see *The FT Essential Guide to Writing a Business Plan*
- Risk, opportunity and sensitivity (Chapter 9)
- Action plan – over the next three to five years.

This plan can be in either document or slide form. The latter is preferable, as long as it forces the strategist to use fewer words. A slide crammed full of words is a no-no – it is unreadable on screen and infuriating to the people you are trying to convince. That number of words is better off as a document.

Or it can be both – a detailed document for analysis by managers, a summary presentation in slide form for the board.

In the detailed document, try to keep the main body to a minimum. Restrict analysis of market demand, for example, to one or two pages – and put the supporting detail in an appendix. Build up a dozen or more appendices on supporting evidence and analysis.

When presenting to the board, a guiding principle should be 'less is

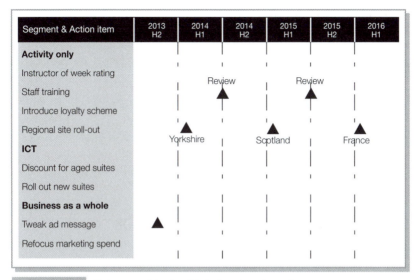

Segment & Action item	2013 H2	2014 H1	2014 H2	2015 H1	2015 H2	2016 H1
Activity only						
Instructor of week rating						
Staff training			Review ▲		Review ▲	
Introduce loyalty scheme						
Regional site roll-out		▲ Yorkshire		▲ Scotland		▲ France
ICT						
Discount for aged suites						
Roll out new suites						
Business as a whole						
Tweak ad message	▲					
Refocus marketing spend						

Figure 10.1 Extramural Ltd: a high-level action plan

more'. Keep the slides to few words, plenty of graphics. Stick to the big picture. Talk around the slides, not to them.

The action plan should be high-level. A simple Gantt chart for each business unit should suffice, with rows denoting key action elements of the strategy and columns the time units (years, half-years or quarters, as opposed to months or weeks) – see the example for Extramural Ltd in Figure 10.1, which builds on the profit growth initiatives shown in Table 7.3. For the board, one summary Gantt chart for the company as a whole, with rows denoting major business unit initiatives and columns the broad time units, might be sufficient.

Further levels of detail may well be needed to ensure successful strategy implementation, but that belongs more to the realm of project planning, where the Gantt chart columns may denote months or weeks – even, for some projects, days.

During the economic downturn of 1991, a gathering of automotive executives met in Detroit and opined memorably: 'We strategize beautifully, but implement pathetically'.

Don't be like them. Translate your strategy into action – and the first step in enacting strategy is the strategic plan, in turn leading to a high level action plan.

Reviewing the plan

Monitoring and evaluating the strategic plan is a key component of a systematised strategic planning process – see Chapter 11 and Figure 11.1.

But such a process belongs more to a large company than to an SME. What if your firm has only drawn up a strategic plan on an *ad hoc* basis? Should it be monitored or evaluated?

Yes and yes. If you have taken all that trouble, effort, time and perhaps expense to draw up a strategy and incorporate it into a strategic plan, then you should at least do yourself the honour of keeping an eye on how that plan turns out.

If your strategic plan was drawn up for purposes of a transaction, your backer may well want to be kept informed on the progress of key parameters – not just the P&L and cash position on a monthly basis, but key sales value, volume and margin data, progress on capital expenditure items, marketing initiatives, etc.

If these parameters vary significantly from what was forecast, why? If the variation is adverse, how can the impact be lessened, even turned round?

Monitoring is important in the first year of a strategic plan. Beyond that it may become usurped by the annual budgetary process. By the third year, the document is history.

Monitoring, by then, is no longer relevant, but evaluation certainly is. And for one good reason. Think of all that investment of time and effort that went into the creation of the strategic plan. You may have to do it again, perhaps sometime soon. What can you do better next time? What lessons can be learnt from last time?

Did market demand turn out as forecast? Was competition as tough as expected? Was competitor A's anticipated new product launch as successful as had been feared? Did that marketing campaign really catch fire? Should we have withdrawn earlier from country/region F? How could we have finished that plant extension sooner? Did we raise prices sufficiently on product D?

Could significant deviations from plan have been foreseen? To what extent could we have done things differently during the strategic planning process to improve our chances of getting these assumptions right?

This is the benefit of evaluation. It is not to praise those who made the right calls and scorn those who got it wrong. It is to try to learn lessons about how the strategic planning process can work better for you next time.

11

The strategic planning process

" In preparing for battle I have always found that plans are useless, but planning is indispensable.

Dwight D. Eisenhower

In this chapter

- Strategic planning in a multi-business corporation
  - Essential tool: Deliberate vs emergent strategy
- Strategic planning in a medium-sized enterprise
- Strategic planning in a small company
- Strategic planning for a start-up

The drawing up of a strategic plan may be a one-off, a sporadic exercise, undertaken as required, often for transactional purposes.

Or it can be built into your company's planning system. Thus strategy development can be carried out regularly, whether annually in the months before the budgetary planning process or on, say, a three-yearly basis. This is strategic planning.

Most large, multi-business companies carry out strategic planning. Most small companies do not. Medium-sized companies sit in between – some do, most don't.

To the proponents of strategic planning, the benefits in preparation, mobilisation of resources and organisational control are obvious. Its detractors acknowledge such benefits but see them outweighed by the negatives, in particular the motivation-sapping bureaucracy and the stifling of creativity and innovation.

Let us look first at how strategic planning works in a large organisation, then we shall see how applicable it is to small and medium-sized firms.

Strategic planning in a multi-business corporation

If General Eisenhower thought that planning was indispensable, who are we to argue? And yet he found the resultant plans useless. Let's examine this further.

The merits of planning in military strategy lie primarily in resource mobilisation and deployment. Without planning, an army will not have the right troops, with the right training, munitions and supplies, in the right place at the right time.

But the ultimate, detailed plan of campaign, for engaging in combat with the enemy, may, in Eisenhower's words, be useless. The fighting itself depends as much on the initiative and valour of the combatants as on the strategy that put them there in the first place.

He exaggerates to make the point. Some military strategies, like those of Admiral Nelson at the Battle of Trafalgar or General Giap at the Battle of Dien Bien Phu, were brilliant in their conception and their execution.

But even in those decisive engagements the implementation would not have been exactly as planned – the plans assigned to an individual commander whose ship took an early cannon ball to the mainmast might have been useless, but the planning that delivered the resources and their deployment to the battle was indispensable.

Which is why most large organisations find a systematised strategic planning process indispensable. Most have a specified strategy unit, with a Director of Strategy, reporting either to the CFO or directly to the CEO. They are not line managers, they take no direct responsibility for businesses or product/market segments, nor do they manage many employees. They are thinkers, analysts, strategists – and communicators, for strategic planning can only be as successful as the communication and harmonious interaction between strategists and line managers.

The strategic plans they draw up each year are designed to guide corporate HQ in their all-important decisions on resource allocation – just as for General Eisenhower or Admiral Nelson. Which resources go where, and why.

They are also about coordination. The strategists act as orchestrators of an information gathering, analysing and sharing process throughout the organisation. They ensure that all are singing from the same hymn sheet.

Strategic plans can also be a key ingredient in the performance assessment of managers. Performance metrics can be directly linked to strategic aims. Managers can be incentivised towards the attainment of these targets.

Corporate planning and control used to be more top-down, with targets drawn up and resources distributed from above. Central corporate control over the allocation of resources was seen as paramount. Corporate management effectively assumed responsibility for business-level as well as corporate-level performance.

This centralised approach led to mixed results and much criticism. These days a more bottom-up approach to planning and control is customary. Corporate HQ issues guidelines only, leaving business-level managers to draw up draft business plans for their businesses – to be discussed, tweaked and finalised in discussion with corporate strategists and the finance department. These business plans are then brought together in an overall corporate strategic plan and budget and submitted to the board for approval.

Performance targets will be set by both corporate and business-level managers, the plan will be monitored, reviewed and evaluated by dedicated personnel, their findings will be fed back to the business-level managers, and the annual cycle of strategic planning will recommence (see Figure 11.1).

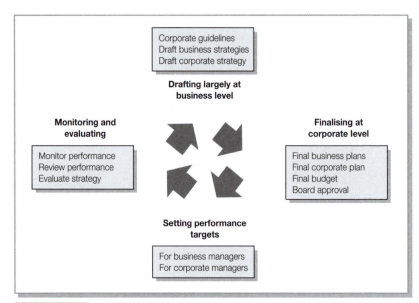

Figure 11.1 A standard strategic planning cycle

This structure addresses some of the more obvious weaknesses of the strategic planning process. Business-level managers, not HQ, draft the plans for their strategic business units. These managers take full responsibility for their implementation. Plans are thus drafted by those closest to their markets and implemented by those who stand to gain or lose most from their delivery.

And yet even this evolved strategic planning system has its critics. Henry Mintzberg, the iconoclastic Canadian professor, sees this system as still over-centralised and insufficiently intuitive – see the essential tool text box. Strategy should not be deliberate, it should be emergent. It should respond to events as they unfold, with managers continually testing the market, probing for opportunities, taking risks – all without the deadening hand of the bureaucratic strategist reclining comfortably, far from the coalface, in corporate HQ.

Strategic planning has had its day, says Mintzberg, it has risen and fallen. Systematised strategic planning is simply too cumbersome a process to equip today's corporations in a world of technological change.

His arguments of 1994 may seem even more valid today. Technological change has accelerated this century. Planning horizons have become ever shorter. Even old-tech companies like the oil majors have lowered their planning horizons, from five to two years.

Facebook is the ultimate example. It is a company that evolved into a multi-billion giant without structure, without plans, without rules. Its brilliance was to allow the market to dictate its path. Suck it and see was its unwritten strategy. Meanwhile its predecessor and rival, MySpace, was acquired by News Corporation, absorbed into a systematised strategic planning process and faded away. Mintzberg 2 Strategic Planning 0, one might argue.

Yes and no. You should take care with Mintzbergian strategy. Taken to its extreme, emergent strategy equals no strategy – just flying by the seat of the pants.

On the deliberate-emergent strategy spectrum, veer towards the emergent if yours is a company in a fast-changing environment, especially if technology-driven. But for companies in more mature industries, you should opt more towards the deliberate – albeit retaining sufficient flexibility to accommodate emergent trends at business level.

Remember: the planning process may be indispensible.

Essential tool

Deliberate vs emergent strategy

Is strategic planning too restrictive, too structured, too analytical, too centralised, done by too many people? Clever, yes, but unblooded, unexposed to the front line?

Would strategy not be better conducted by line managers, responding to events as they unfold, as they see them, taking risks, testing the market, probing for opportunities?

Strategy should be as much emergent as deliberate, says Henry Mintzberg. Strategic planning remains useful, but it needs to be:

■ more decentralised;
■ more intuitive.

It is better done by managers than by strategists. Five-year plans can be out of date within a couple of years in mature industries or before the ink has dried in technology industries.

Industry boundaries have become more fluid. The value chain is more dispersed and more shared. 'Black Swan' events (see Chapter 9) throw plans off course more frequently. Industry analysis can be redundant, even misleading.

Firms need to be fleet of foot, strategically flexible. Organisations need to be structured as an 'adhocracy', the diametric opposite of a bureaucracy, with flat lines of responsibility, decentralised decision-making and small-team project work, with appropriate liaison mechanisms.

Strategy should emerge over time as intentions collide with and respond to a changing reality.

This is emergent strategy. It is what works in practice, says Mintzberg.

Strategic planning in a medium-sized enterprise

I did some work for a privately owned European company turning over around €200m in the packaging sector a couple of years ago. I was surprised but initially delighted to find that they had built a strategic planning system into their annual budgetary process.

Each year managers of the business units would update the sections on market demand, competition and business development and tweak the business strategy accordingly. This analysis would feed into the annual budget and three-year financial forecasts.

In theory this worked well. A medium-sized company, advised by some persuasive consultant a few years previously to adopt the strategic planning system pertinent to a much larger company, was producing results that looked most impressive, in both the Excel model and the PowerPoint presentation.

The trouble was that people did not believe the results. No one did. Not the line managers who drafted them, nor the corporate managers who reviewed them. Certainly not the company's financiers.

The only set of numbers that managers believed in was the annual budget. This was hard fought over. Business managers loaded the numbers with conservatism, corporate managers grilled them and tried to raise them to more ambitious targets.

Both sets of managers knew that their performance would be measured in terms of outcome versus budget. They may not even be around to be measured against numbers achieved in Year 3 of the strategic plan.

Corporate managers enjoyed the PowerPoint presentations of the annually updated business strategies, but did not dig too deep. What was of greater importance and more time consuming was the debate later on the annual budget – so the sooner the slideshow was over, the better.

This is not to criticise the company. It is to point out the inadvisability of loading a medium-sized firm with a planning system designed for a company with far greater resources.

The reason why corporate managers were disinterested in the strategy updates was because they did not believe them. They knew that the business-level managers had done no primary research and minimal secondary research to produce them. Managers had just taken the documents from the previous year, amended some numbers and dates and added a bullet point here and there on a slide or two to make it seem more contemporary.

There is an important lesson here. A half-hearted strategic planning system is useless, indeed worse. It is potentially misleading – and could lead to the wrong strategic decisions being made on resource allocation.

In this example, that latter eventuality was unlikely – since no one in HQ believed the strategy, nor the three-year forecasts.

But in other cases it will not be so clear cut. A new CEO might inherit the system and instruct his business-level managers to do the research and produce meaningful results. Some will be capable of doing that, others won't. Some will want to do it, others won't. Some will put aside the time to do it, others won't. Some corporate managers will believe the results, others won't.

There is an admirable maxim in IT: garbage in, garbage out. So too in strategic planning.

If strategic planning is worth doing, it should be done properly. The research should be undertaken, the analysis carried through.

It is unacceptably risky to undertake a strategy review without going to the marketplace and finding out directly what is going on. That means talking to customers, suppliers, competitors, industry observers – and not in some random manner, but within the context of a structured interview programme (see the Appendix to this book).

Market data needs proper gathering and analysis, so too competitor data – on strategy, employees, assets, sales, profitability.

All this is time consuming and expensive, especially as it will involve significant amounts of senior manager time.

The average medium-sized firm does not have the resources nor the management time to carry out strategic planning satisfactorily every year. Instead it should be done on a fixed period basis or *ad hoc*.

It could be undertaken, say, every three years – but done properly. The plan would have a name and a date attached, like ABC Ltd Strategic Plan, 2013–16. Managers and financiers could then use that document in confidence in 2014, knowing that it had been done properly in 2013, and with an element of confidence in 2015–16, knowing that it had been done properly at the time but was becoming a little out of date.

Even better, ABC Ltd could include in its annual budget a section on a Review of the Strategic Plan, updating the reader on trends in the market and at the firm and how things have changed since the plan.

Or strategic plans could be drawn up on an *ad hoc* basis, as and when required – typically for transactional purposes, whether for raising external finance or transfer of ownership (see below for small companies).

In summary, strategic planning in a medium-sized enterprise should be treated with care. It is seldom that such a company will have the resources to do the job properly each year. A plan every three years or on an *ad hoc* basis may be the answer.

Strategic planning in a small company

A small company should have a strategy, but not a systematised strategic planning process.

The strategy may or may not be formally articulated – many business people have strategies residing in the mind of the owner, which may be perfectly valid. But it helps to clarify woolly thinking and to bring on board the management team if it is written down.

A small company should not have an annual or periodic strategic planning process – management time is far better spent winning new custom or ensuring that existing customers are super-pleased with the product and/or service.

But a strategic plan may well be needed for transactional purposes.

If your small business is in need of finance and you already have a well-defined strategy, you will need a business plan (see this book's companion guide, *The FT Essential Guide to Writing a Business Plan: How to Win Backing to Start Up or Grow Your Business*). In a critical chapter of the business plan, you will articulate your strategy – see the contents of a business plan in Chapter 10.

If you don't have a well-defined strategy, you will need to develop one in line with Part One of this book. To maximise your chances of obtaining backing, your strategy and business plan must be robust and rooted in a coherent, comprehensive and convincing analysis of the market environment and your firm's competitiveness.

A prime example of when a strategy is needed for a small firm on an *ad hoc* basis is shown in the central case study of this book – Extramural Ltd. The company has an annual budgeting process, but no strategic planning system.

The Davieses hadn't undertaken a formal strategy process since the early days when they needed some external equity finance. Now they want to be in a position to exit the company in five years' time, so they seek a strategy to maximise the potential of the company by then.

They know too that they will have to revisit their strategy in four to five years' time in order to draw up a strategy for the new owners to buy into. This will again need to be a fully researched and analysed strategy – they may well engage another graduate intern to do the nitty gritty. This updated strategy will form the basis of the business plan that will be sent out by their corporate finance advisers to potential bidders, including private equity houses. The latter will engage consultants highly specialised in strategic due diligence, who will forensically examine every assumption in the business plan. It will have to be fireproof.

That is why rigorous strategy development will be needed, feeding into a coherent business plan. If a strategic plan is defined as strategy + business plan = strategic plan, the Davieses know that only a thoroughly robust strategic plan will deliver them in five years' time the rewards they believe to be their due after 25 years of dedication to the business.

Strategic planning for a start-up

The requirement for strategic planning for a start-up is little different than for a small established enterprise like Extramural Ltd.

It is needed only on an *ad hoc* basis – for transactional purposes or for transfer of ownership. Otherwise no strategic planning is necessary.

But remember that the strategic plan shown to seed or venture capitalists will need to work harder to be convincing. You will have no track record.

You will have to marshal whatever evidence you can glean to demonstrate the very existence of market demand, your distinctive offering and the sustainability of your competitive advantage to convince the backer.

But do the research, conduct the analysis and present this once-off, *ad hoc* strategic plan and you will greatly enhance your chances of winning the backing you need for your business to succeed.

Conclusion

You now have a strategy to guide your firm to the next level.

The process wasn't that grim, was it?

Your firm is now far better equipped for the future than it was before.

Michael Porter once wrote that 'the company without a strategy is willing to try anything'.

Not yours. It will have direction. You will be facing the future with a strategy which will maximise your chances of achieving your goals.

You have the strategy you need for your business to succeed.

Appendix: Structured interviewing

A structured interviewing programme of customers, suppliers, competitors and industry observers is the essential research for a strategy development process. It is the most methodical and potentially enlightening way to obtain the basic information needed to derive your firm's competitive position – and from there to draw up your business strategy.

Here's how to do structured interviewing of customers:

- Select a representative range of interviewees.
- Prepare your storyline.
- Prepare a concise questionnaire.
- Interview them, through email, telephone or face-to-face.
- Thank them and give them some feedback.

The interviewees

The interviewees should represent a broad cross-section of your business, including:

- Customers from each of your main business segments
- Your top six customers in terms of revenue
- Long-standing customers as well as recent acquisitions
- Customers who also use, or used to use, your competitors, so they can compare your performance from direct experience rather than conjecture
- Customers with whom you've had problems
- Would-be customers, currently using a competitor, but on your target list
- Former customers who switched to a competitor – these can potentially yield the most valuable insights of all.

That sounds like a lot, but you'll be selective. Three to six customers for each main segment should suffice, two dozen or so per business in all.

The storyline

Here's your opportunity to put a positive light on your business. Compare these two storylines:

1 'Sorry to waste your time but can I ask for your help in figuring out how well our firm performs?'

2 'As you know, our firm has been rather busy over the last couple of years. But we thought we should take some time out to ask some of our most important customers how their needs may be changing over time and to what extent we can serve those needs better.'

Guess which line will get the better response *and* put your business in a favourable light? The first storyline conveys a negative impression and is all about your firm and its needs. The second leaves a positive impression and is all about your customer's needs. Stick to the second!

The questionnaire

The questionnaire needs care. It must be taken as a guideline, not as a box-ticking exercise. It stays with you, and it doesn't get handed or emailed to the interviewee. It's a prompter to discussion, no more. It needs to be simple. And concise.

It should be in four parts:

1 The storyline

2 Customer purchasing criteria – which, how important, now and in the future?

3 Performance – how your firm and your competitors rate against those purchasing criteria.

4 The future – how you can better serve your customer's needs.

The storyline

The storyline should be written out at the top of the questionnaire and memorised. It must be delivered naturally and seemingly spontaneously. Stick in the odd pause, 'um' or 'er' to make it seem less rehearsed.

Customer purchasing criteria

These are the main questions to put on your questionnaire:

- What are your main criteria in buying this service? What do you expect from your providers?
- How important are each of these criteria? Which are more important than others? How would you rank them?
- Will these criteria become more or less important over time?
- Are any other criteria likely to become important in the future?

You should allow the customer to draw up her own set of criteria, but it's best to prepare your own list to use as prompts, in case your customer dries up or misses an obvious one.

Performance

Here are some performance-related questions:

- How do you think our firm meets those criteria? How do we perform?
- How do other providers perform? Do they better meet those criteria?
- Who performs best against those most important criteria?

Again you should allow the customer to select who she thinks are her alternative providers, but you should include a prompt list of your main competitors – which you may or may not choose to use. No need to alert her to a troublesome competitor she's not fully aware of!

The future

What should we be doing to better meet your needs and those of other customers?

The interview

Interviews are best done face-to-face. Then you can see the nuances behind the replies – the shifting glance, the fidgeting, the emphatic hand gestures. But they are the most time consuming, unless you happen to be seeing your customer as part of your service delivery anyway.

If the interviews are done over the phone, they are best scheduled in advance. You can do this by email or with a preliminary phone call. After you've delivered the storyline, then add: 'I wonder if you could spare five to ten minutes to discuss this with me. I know you're very busy, but perhaps we could set up a time later in the week for me to give you a call.'

The call itself must be carefully managed. Don't launch into the questionnaire without a warm-up. Ask her how she's doing, how's work, how's the family, whatever. Then gently shift to the storyline: 'Well, as I was saying the other day ...'.

After you've finished the structured interview, don't forget the warm-down at the closing. Return to one of the topics you discussed at the outset and gently wind down the discussion, not forgetting to thank her sincerely for giving so freely of her valuable time.

The thanks and feedback

A few hours, a day, a couple of days, or a week later – whenever you feel it's appropriate – thank your customer again, officially. By letter is best, but that may feel too formal for you in this electronic world. Email is probably fine, but use your judgement.

The email should be cheerful and full of sincere gratitude. If possible, it should contain a snippet of information that could be of interest or use to your customer. One or two sentences should suffice. It could pick up on one aspect of the discussion and compare what another customer had to say on the same thing. You could give her an indication of the results of your survey: 'Interestingly, most customers seemed to think that track record was their most important need' or 'Encouragingly, most customers seemed to think we were the most innovative service provider!'.

That's structured interviewing. Now all you have to do is compile the results, whether on a piece of paper, on an Excel worksheet, or simply in your head, and feed them into your ratings against each KSF – for your firm and for each of your main competitors.

The intriguing thing then is to compare these customer-derived ratings with your first draft, do-it-yourself ratings. You may be in for a surprise!

Structured interviewing of suppliers follows the same process – selecting a range of interviewees, preparing the storyline and a questionnaire, interviewing and feeding back.

Here are a couple of tips:

- Supplier interviews can be an important source of information on your competitors; you are not asking them to furnish you with confidential information on their customers, but they may well know of information that is in the public domain but that you were unaware of – for example, that a competitor had shifted production of one product line from plant A to plant B, or that another competitor was now buying in all supplies of one component from the Far East and no longer using national suppliers.

- Choose the list of suppliers to be interviewed not necessarily on grounds of scale of supplies to your firm, but on how much they are likely to know about what is happening in the industry and, in particular, with your competitors.

Structured interviewing of competitors is trickier. You can't really call them up directly and say who you are, let alone leave your firm's telephone number on their voicemail and ask them to return your call!

You may need to hand the task to a third party, whether a paid consultant or unpaid friend.

Keep it ethical. Your third party is conducting a market survey, using publicly available information, period. This must not be an underhand means to elicit proprietary information out of the company.

You are rather giving your competitor the opportunity to express its views in two main areas:

- The market as a whole – where it is going, what is driving it – answers to the same questions as would be asked by a journalist from a trade magazine calling round to get industry participants' views on the direction of the market.
- The company's sales pitch – why it is distinctive, why it is better than the competition's, why it will be even better in the future – the same pitch it gives to a would-be customer who shows up at its stall at a trade show.

Much of this information will be old hat, most of it bland. But useful insights always come out of competitor calls – even if they are just confirmation of your own views.

Structured interviewing of industry observers, whether market researchers, trade journalists, university lecturers or civil servants, should likewise be structured in advance. You must know what you want to get out of the interview before you knock on the door or pick up the phone. The focus will again be on industry-wide issues and trends, but, you never know, you may learn one or two intriguing things about the competition too as you go along.

Essential tip

Take care not to waste customers' time. Try to ensure they too get something useful out of the meeting.

Further reading

Chapter 1: Knowing your business

Richard Koch, *The 80/20 Principle, The Secret of Achieving More with Less*, Nicholas Brealey Publishing, 2nd edition, 2007

Chapter 2: Setting goals and objectives

James C. Collins and Jerry I. Porras, *Built to Last: Successful Habits of Visionary Companies*, Random House, 1997

Chapter 3: Forecasting market demand

John Mullins, *The New Business Road Test: What Entrepreneurs and Executives Should Do Before Writing a Business Plan*, FT Prentice Hall, 3rd edition, 2010

Chapter 4: Gauging industry competition

Michael E. Porter, *Competitive Strategy: Techniques for Analyzing Industries and Competitors*, Free Press, 1980

Chapter 5: Tracking competitive advantage

Robert M. Grant, *Contemporary Strategy Analysis*, Blackwell, 7th edition, 2011

Michael E. Porter, *Competitive Advantage*, Free Press, 1984

Chapter 6: Targeting the strategic gap

Gary Hamel and C. K. Prahalad, *Competing for the Future*, Harvard Business School Press, 1994

Richard Koch, *The FT Guide to Strategy: How to Create, Pursue and Deliver a Winning Strategy*, FT Prentice Hall, 4th edition, 2011

Chapter 7: Bridging the gap: business strategy

Jim Collins, *Good to Great: Why Some Companies Make the Leap … and Others Don't*, Random House Business, 2001

Vaughan Evans, *Key Strategy Tools: The 80+ Tools for Every Manager to Build a Winning Strategy*, FT Publishing, 2013

W. Chan Kim and Renee Mauborgne, *Blue Ocean Strategy: How to Create Uncontested Market Space and Make the Competition Irrelevant*, Harvard Business School Press, 2005

Tim Koller, Marc Goedhart and David Wessels (all McKinsey & Co.), *Valuation: Measuring and Managing the Value of Companies*, 5th edition, 2010

Chapter 8: Bridging the gap: corporate strategy

Clayton M. Christensen, *The Innovator's Dilemma: When New Technologies Cause Great Firms to Fail*, Harvard Business School Press, 1997

David J. Collis and Cynthia A. Montgomery, *Competing on Resources: Strategy in the 1990s*, Harvard Business Review, July–August 1995, reprinted as *Competing on Resources*, July 2008

Michael Goold, Andrew Campbell and Marcus Alexander, *Corporate-Level Strategy: Creating Value in Multi-Business Companies*, Wiley, 1994

Linda Gratton, *Innovation Hot Spots: Why Some Companies Buzz with Energy and Innovation … and Others Don't*, FT Prentice Hall, 2007

Richard P. Rumelt, *Good Strategy, Bad Strategy: The Difference and Why It Matters*, Profile, 2011

Chris Zook, *Profit from the Core*, Harvard Business Press, 2001

Chapter 9: Addressing risk and opportunity

Vaughan Evans, *Backing U!: A Business-Oriented Guide to Backing Your Passion and Achieving Career Success*, Business and Careers Press, 2009

Nassim Nicholas Taleb, *The Black Swan: The Impact of the Highly Improbable*, Allen Lane, 2007

Chapter 10: The strategic plan

Vaughan Evans, *The FT Essential Guide to Writing a Business Plan: How to Win Backing to Start Up or Grow Your Business*, FT Publishing, 2011

Chapter 11: The strategic planning process

Henry Mintzberg, *The Rise and Fall of Strategic Planning*, Free Press, 1994

Glossary

Advantage See competitive advantage.

Attractiveness See market attractiveness.

'Benchmarking' A systematic approach to measuring key metrics in a firm's operations, systems and processes against best practice, whether found in the same industry or others.

'Black Swan event' A very rare event, one of such magnitude and improbability that people choose to ignore it, yet explicable and justifiable with hindsight.

'Blue oceans' Uncontested market space, as distinct from the 'red oceans' of existing market space.

Brainstorming A structured process for the generation of ideas, done individually or in a group setting.

Business Strategic business unit.

Business process redesign (or re-engineering) Radical, comprehensive rethinking of key business processes to attain step-up levels of cost, production, quality, speed or service performance.

Business strategy Gaining a sustainable competitive advantage in a single strategic business unit.

Capabilities How a firm deploys its resources.

Capability gap The gap in performance between where your firm is currently positioned against key success factors and where it aims to be.

Competitive advantage The strategic advantage possessed by one firm over others in a product/market segment or industry which enables it to make superior returns.

Competitive intensity   The degree of competition in a given industry and a main determinant of industry profitability.

Competitive position   A rating of a firm's relative competitiveness in a given product/market segment or business.

Complement   The opposite of a substitute – where an increase in demand for one good (or service) results in an increase in demand for another.

Core competence   An integrated bundle of skills and technologies, the sum of learning across individual skill sets and individual organisational units.

Corporate social responsibility   How firms address the social, environmental and economic impacts of their operations and so help meet sustainable development goals.

Corporate strategy   Optimising value from a portfolio of businesses and adding value to each through exploiting the firm's core resources and capabilities.

Customer purchasing criteria ('CPCs')   What customers need from their suppliers.

Discounted cash flow analysis   Projected annual cash inflows less outflows, including the upfront capital outflow, discounted at the opportunity cost of capital and summed to yield a net present value.

Economies of scale   The reduction in unit costs in a firm arising from an increase in the scale of its operations.

Economies of scope   The reduction in unit costs in a firm arising from the production of similar or related goods or services.

Expected value   The parameter value multiplied by the probability of that value being realised.

Experience curve   An effect whereby the unit cost of a standard product declines by a constant percentage each time cumulative output doubles.

The five forces   Michael Porter's key forces driving industry competition, namely internal rivalry, the threat of new entrants or substitutes and supplier and customer bargaining power.

Generic strategies   Those which relate to an entire genus or class, namely differentiation, low-cost or focus strategies.

HOOF approach   Forecasting market demand by assessing the historic (H) rate of growth, identifying key drivers (D), assessing how these and potentially new drivers may change in the future (D) and thereby deriving demand forecasts (F).

Ideal player   The theoretical competitor who achieves the highest possible rating against each key success factor.

Industry maturity   The stage of evolution of an industry, from embryonic through to growing, mature and ageing.

Industry supply   The aggregate supply by producers of a product (or product group) over a specified period of time, typically one year.

Issue   A matter under discussion or in dispute, often due to future uncertainty – a risk or an opportunity.

Key success factors ('KSFs')   What firms need to do to both meet customer purchasing criteria and run a sound business.

Macro-economics   The study of the aggregate economy, whether regional, national or international.

Market attractiveness   A composite measure of the relative attractiveness of a product/market segment, taking into account factors such as market size, market growth, competitive intensity, industry profitability and market risk.

Market contextual plan review   An assessment of the achievability of the revenues and margins forecast in a business plan by key product/market segment.

'Marketcrafting'   Creating estimates of market size (and growth) and market share (and growth) from the bottom up, by using index numbers to gauge the relative scale of key producers, present and past.

Market demand   The aggregate demands of customers for a product (or product group) over a specified period of time, typically one year.

Market-positioning school   Proponents of the view that strategy should be focused at the level of the business, where all meaningful competition resides, and corporate strategy limited to portfolio planning.

Micro-economics   The study of small economic units, such as the consumer, the household, the non-profit organisation or, most commonly, the firm.

Moving average   A method of smoothing a time series (typically annual) by averaging a fixed number of consecutive terms (typically three years).

Net present value   The end-result of discounted cash flow analysis.

Offshoring   Outsourcing carried out by foreign, usually lower-cost suppliers.

Outsourcing   The process of buying in business processes from independent providers as opposed to performing them in-house.

The 4Ps   The product, place, price and promotion components of the marketing mix.

Parenting advantage   The creation of synergies not just between strategic business units but between them and the centre.

Payback   The number of years it takes for net cash inflows to recoup initial investment costs.

Portfolio   The collection of key product/market segments in a business or of businesses in a multi-business company.

Resource-based school   Proponents of the view that strategy should be focused on leveraging the resources and capabilities of the corporation as a whole.

Resources   A firm's productive assets, whether human, physical, financial or intangible, as distinct from capabilities, which are how a firm deploys such resources.

Scenario   A coherent and consistent portrayal of a series of future events based on specific parameter assumptions made by the strategist.

Segment   A slice of business where the firm sells one product (or product group) to one customer group strictly a 'product/market segment' or 'business segment'.

Sensitivity analysis   The tweaking of parameter value assumptions to test overall impact on key financials.

Shareholder value   The value a shareholder gains from investing in a firm through dividend and other payouts and capital appreciation/gain upon exit.

SMART objectives   Those which are specific, measurable, attainable, relevant and time-limited.

SMEs   Small and medium-sized enterprises.

Stakeholder   Persons and organisations with a non-shareholding stake in the success of the firm, for example employees, customers, suppliers, national and local government, the local community.

Strategically valuable resources   Those which are valuable only if recognised strategically within an industry/market context.

Strategic business unit ('SBU')   A profit centre entity with a closely interrelated product (or service) offering and a cost structure largely independent of other business units.

Strategic due diligence (aka market or commercial due diligence)   An assessment of the key risks and opportunities in market demand, industry competition, competitive position, strategy and business prospects facing a target company.

Strategic investment decision   Go/no-go decision on an investment of strategic importance.

Strategic repositioning   Adjusting strategic position through investing, holding, exiting or entering segments (for business strategy) or businesses (for corporate strategy).

Strategy   How a firm achieves its goals by deploying its scarce resources to gain a sustainable competitive advantage.

Structured interviewing   Systematised interviewing of customers, suppliers, competitors and other industry observers to gain strategic information.

Substitute   The opposite of a complement – where an increase in demand for one good or service results in a decrease in demand for another.

Suns & clouds chart   An assessment of key risks and opportunities, portrayed visually as suns and clouds, by likelihood of occurrence and value impact.

Synergy   Where the whole is greater than the sum of the parts and, specifically in mergers, acquisitions and alliances, where the value of the merged entity is greater than the pre-bid stand-alone value of the acquirer plus that of the target (or partner).

Value chain   The key primary and support activities of a firm.

Index

More from Vaughan Evans